The Super Easy Guide to Job Searching and Resume Sculpting

The Super Easy Guide to Job Searching and Resume Sculpting

Enjoy Your Life,
Enjoy Your Work:
The Simplified Course

Andrea Charlotte Angell

The Super Easy Guide to Job Searching and Resume Sculpting
Enjoy Your Life, Enjoy Your Work: The Simplified Course

iUniverse books may be ordered through booksellers or by contacting:

iUniverse
1663 Liberty Drive
Bloomington, IN 47403
www.iuniverse.com
1-800-Authors (1-800-288-4677)

ISBN: 978-1-4759-2855-6 (sc)
ISBN: 978-1-4759-2856-3 (e)

Print information available on the last page.

iUniverse rev. date: 02/26/2016

Dedication

To everyone who is searching for employment and especially to Tom, who made me promise to write a book for those people, namely his son, who can't make it to my class in person because they live too far away but who are struggling and need help with their job search.

Acknowledgements

I am deeply grateful to all of my students and friends whose stories inspire me daily!

A special thank you to Katherine Augade for her incredible energy, love and support!

Based on the Job Search Coaching and Resume Sculpting Course
Instructed by, Andrea Charlotte Angell

Make the Right Impression!

Table of contents

Chapter 6
Resume sculpting

Chapter 7
Interviews

Chapter 8
Keeping the job

About the Author

Andrea Charlotte Angell has utilized her resume processing skills since 1996 to help job seekers reach their full potential by conducting essential advising on all aspects of the job search.

She has also been a Job Search Coach and Resume Sculpting Instructor since 2007 at the Skyline Campus in Salt Lake City, Utah.

Miss Angell also owns a business called Accelerated Principles where she coaches individuals with their job search and resume sculpting. She knows how hard it can be for job seekers to find work, especially in an unforgiving economy. Her passion is not just to help job seekers find work, but to help them find work where they will remain happy and fulfilled for years to come!

www.AcceleratedPrinciples.com

ENJOY YOUR LIFE

ENJOY YOUR WORK!

Chapter 1

Job Searching

Welcome!

Overview:

We are here to help you figure out what you want in a particular job or career and what a prospective employer may want from you as well. Then you can decide on the greatest matches for you! There will be tips and coaching to help you through the process of attaining the perfect working environment for you.

We will be addressing some key items in this course:

1. **How the job search impacts our emotions and our self-esteem and how we can overcome these obstacles.**
2. **How to figure out what would be the best job or career for you and your lifestyle.**
3. **Organizing your data together to be ready for any application and interview.**
4. **Tips and tricks on how to conduct your job search.**
5. **How to approach companies through various types of initial contacts.**
6. **Composing and targeting your resume effectively.**
7. **How to make the best impression during interview sessions.**
8. **Tips on keeping the job.**

Write things down

Keep a pen and paper handy because as we discuss different topics throughout this course, I want you to write things down that may pertain to you personally even if it seems insignificant at first glance. You will have ideas that come into your mind and you will recall previous experiences that you have had which can be either work related, volunteer experience, military experience, personal experiences as well as hobbies you may have had or now enjoy. Please write these things down as we may be able to incorporate these experiences later into your resume.

Job searching and resume composition helps you take into review every past experience you have had for use with your search for new opportunities. As you recall different experiences, you might remember winning skills to bring up during interview sessions as well. Write it all down! You might be amazed at what you remember and will later be able to incorporate into your noted experiences.

The job search is a full time job

You should be dedicating at least 20 hours a week to your job search if you are not currently employed and are seeking a full time position. You can figure investing approximately four to six hours of your time per day within a five day work week on your search. During these hours your focus will be:

- ◆ Taking the steps every day to search for new employment and researching prospective companies. (Via leads from friends and acquaintances, state employment listings, newspaper listings, internet listings, employment agencies, etc.)
- ◆ Making initial contacts (Making phone calls, passing out cover letters and paper resumes, sending your cyber resume to prospective employers, etc.)
- ◆ Scheduling and attending interviews with prospective employers.
- ◆ Thanking the contact for their time (Via e-mail, follow up letter, etc.)
- ◆ Starting all of these steps over again until you have the job you want!

The average length of unemployment is 3-4 months

Why does it take people so long to find work? The three top reasons:

> ➤ *They are not devoting enough time to the job search.*
> ➤ *They are not communicating effectively either verbally or through their body language.*
> ➤ *They are making a poor impression based on appearance or behavior.*

When the employment rate is higher it is especially important to learn how to compete in the job market. We need to have all the knowledge possible!

Teacher's Objective

Hello, my name is Andrea Angell, my nickname is DRE!

Welcome to the course!

You have chosen to invest some time and education into yourself and I applaud you for that! The job search can be a very challenging part of our lives.

I am here to help you succeed!

In my course I am going to break down all of the misconceptions that make hunting for employment a bit intimidating because truthfully, it doesn't need to be. Try to be open to investing the time for yourself to be able to do all that you need to do to become successful in your search for new employment. I don't want to merely help you find employment, my goal here is to help you find employment where you will be truly happy for years to come. Somewhere where you can feel your worth every day. Where you know that you are valued! That way you will always be happy once you start that new position. Once you make the decision to work at one company or another, you have decided to commit years to working at that particular company, as well as committing a good slice of your day there so I want you to take the time to invest in yourself first and find out what would truly make you happy.

You are top priority right now!

I want to make sure that you are assured and confident before going through the search. I will help you through the process but only you can come to your own conclusions as to which type of employment would best suit your needs as well as fit your individual personality, and there are ways to help you best figure out what would make you the happiest so please don't skip steps! Take some time to invest in yourself.

Tips and Workshops

You will be investing a little time into doing a few worksheets. Any time you invest in yourself like this you will get back all of that and more in the form of confidence, an understanding of yourself and much more! In this course you will first learn more about yourself, and then you will learn techniques to give you confidence during the entire job search process, including the initial contact stage, the interview process, as well as conducting yourself after the interview. You will learn skills that will increase your confidence by learning what to say and what not to say on the application as well as during the interview. I will also let you know the "whys" behind it all so that you have a clear understanding and you may take that knowledge with you for the rest of your life. You may even choose to help other people who may be struggling with their search!

ALL I NEED TO KNOW IS...

I have noticed that when I teach classes, some students in the first week like to just focus on one part of the search such as: "I just need to know what to say during an interview and I am good to go," or they might think, "I just need to get my resume in order and that's all I need." This narrow way of thinking can be detrimental to your success because there are many things that you can learn that will help you so that you are not wasting your time on the job search, or on interviews that are not effective, as well as making sure that you are presenting yourself in the best way possible. This can all lead to more effective use of your time as well as higher consideration for employment and income offered.

Don't skip through the course- Invest some time into yourself!

Do not skip through the course finding only what you think is helpful to you at this time. I want to help you as a whole person, and guide you through the entire job search process, not just any one particular part of it. Invest the time in yourself because you are absolutely worth every minute! I know you don't have a lot of time right now with your search because either you are currently searching for employment, or you are in a job or career that isn't working for you so I will explain the value of a little time investment.

All I need to know is what to say during the interview

Let's address some of these statements for a minute. If you say to yourself: "All I need to know is what to say during an interview," it doesn't make sense to me as this person is not realizing that there are many ways to get to that point, if you know all about what you are going to say during an interview but have no interviews because you skipped over those first crucial steps on how to get an interview scheduled, that may be why you are not getting the opportunity to show off your interview skills! What good is it to know exactly what you will say during an interview if you have no interview appointments?

All I need to know is how to get my resume in order

Let's take the next statement, if you tell yourself, "I just need to get my resume in order and that's all I need." I happen to see this one more than any other statement made. I tell them, "What good is it if you look great on paper and then get to the interview and crash?" I need to instruct you as a whole person for you to gain the maximum results. It is entirely in your hands if you choose to go the lazy route, it will ultimately and intuitively be picked up somewhere by your potential employer and you may not get the employment you seek. You are an adult and no one will be over your shoulder telling you that you have to do the steps to get there. My recommendation therefore, is to not skip around, go through all of the steps, one by one and let me help you help yourself. If you can, give yourself a few days to stop your search and focus on your instruction, then the job search will become a natural full time job for you and you can search with confidence like you have never had before!

YOU'RE WORTH THE INVESTMENT!

Some of the things you learn in this course can even be helpful with making decisions in other areas of your life as well. Give yourself what you need, including time and plenty of encouragement. You are your own best friend! I am going to throw in a lot of my own quirks and stories so that you can see how I work with my challenges as well as my qualities. This will give you better insight to yourself so that you may get more ideas of what I, as well as others, do to magnify our talents that we all naturally possess. Just a bit of study, pondering, organization and of course, effort will help you achieve maximum results! The more effort you put into this course, the more effort you are investing into yourself and therefore the more confident and ready you will be for any type of employment that you choose to suit you as an individual. I have made the course simple and straightforward to help make it easier for you to succeed.

Read the course with highlighter in hand

Take into account all of the hints and tricks in the course, but there may be some that pertain more to your personal circumstances than others. Highlight anything that makes sense to you and reread the highlighted parts when you get discouraged or if you find the search slowing down for you.

This is one book that I WANT you to mark up as well as write in and tear out a few pages if you need to!

Emergency Job Search Tips

If you are in a critical need to gain employment soon, here are some of the main points that we cover more thoroughly during the job search course. Utilize these hints and you will master the course and have a much better chance of getting the job you want!

These emergency hints are never to take place of actually going through the entire course as there are numerous hints throughout the course that are incredibly useful to assist you with all aspects of your search.

1. In this course, we have what we call a data organizer, which allows you to place all of your data from your former employment into one place. All of those specifics are very handy to have in one place so that you can fill out an application in 5 minutes! You also will not have to figure out the information each time you fill out an application, you can just have it there with you! You may write this in a note pad of your own or you may use the organizer that I have made for you in the course. Include your volunteer experience just as you would your employment as it is counted the same and it also shows amazing personal character to volunteer your time.

2. Network! Network! Network! Contact everyone you know and let them know that you are searching for employment! This is the most effective way of getting a job quick! Employers love to hire people that are referred from trusted individuals. Don't leave anyone out, talk to everyone you know!

3. Choose your five key words that describe yourself through the transferable skills section or some of the other lists that contain really rockin' wording that best describes you. You can use these five words on your jist card and you may place as many of them as you want in your resume as well. Review your five key words before each interview.

4. Your job search is a full time job during the time that you are searching—dedicate at least 20 hours a week to the search if you are unemployed and would like a full time position and dedicate at least 5 hours a week if you are currently employed and are seeking other employment or if you are looking for part time work.

5. Once you have filled out your data organizer you will also make notes in it as to any particular areas, or things pertaining to each job that you have excelled at, review these cool facts before each interview so that you can remember to let the interviewer know of these facts during questioning whenever applicable.

6. Always dress "one up" at the interview, from what is normally expected to be worn at that particular job.

7. Send a thank you note or e-mail after each interview, so that they know that you appreciate them taking their time out to meet with you and that you are still interested in the position. Don't forget to include your contact information again on the thank you note.

8. Give your resume in person whenever possible! Copies sent via e-mail and fax never look as great and you will give your resume a better chance to get looked at as well as get an interview if you give them a nice copy of your resume. Another advantage to leaving your resume in person is that you will have a chance visually to impress them with your presence as well, which can be a tremendous plus if you are personable and look the part!

9. Have 5 or 6 extra resumes on hand at each interview so that if you are interviewed by more than one individual you will be prepared to give each interviewer a copy of your resume.

10. Always bring your own pen, notepad and your completely filled out data organizer with you to each interview and to fill out applications- sounds simple, but you do not want to look silly asking for a pen or something to write on as this will show you as unprepared. If you have copies of written references, bring them as well.

11. Pay attention to detail regarding your clothing even down to your shoes. Make sure that hair and makeup is nice at the same time. Remember, you are giving them a visual impression about yourself that speaks volumes within the first two minutes of meeting you! Hygiene is crucial!

12. Keep your resume to one page only. You may use the front and back only if absolutely necessary.

13. Remember! The interviewer needs you to be the right person just as much as you need the job because they are usually managers who are working overtime to fill the gap of that position being open so *BE* the right person! And relax during the interview.

14. Interviewers want to hire real people that they get along with so try not to be a robot during the interview, allow your personality to come out and have fun! They will remember you as the best candidate even if they have more qualified candidates that are not as personable. This is especially true in fields where you will be working with a lot of associates as well as the general public.

15. When filling out an application, always use the words "open" or "negotiable" on the salary field because if you place an amount that is too high, you may not get the call, and if you place an amount that is too low, you may get offered that amount, but you may have significantly cut down what you would have been offered.

16. It is always up to the interviewer to bring up salary, do not bring it up yourself. After they do bring it up, if you can get them talking about money during an interview, you may inadvertently be offered a certain salary, and in the interviewers mind they have just offered you the job! Do not directly bring it up as you are not desperate. Once they start asking you about desired wage, always place the question back on them. You may instead, ask them questions such as: "What do you think my qualifications are worth?" etc.

17. Keep a time sheet for yourself as to how much time you are investing in your job search and what specific things you are doing for your search. Keep tabs on your time to make sure that you are achieving your goals.

18. Be as flexible as you can regarding your hours of availability, because when you are not able to work the shift the interviewer needs to fill at that particular time, you can be in the "no" pile right away. Once you are in the no pile, employers rarely look over those resumes again when they need another shift or another position filled.

19. Invest the time to do all of the workshop exercises to help you to pinpoint what you are looking for in the employment search that will make you the most happy and fulfilled in your life.

20. Most interviewers are not trained at interviewing, rather they are managers who are trained for the job itself and so please do not get discouraged if they ask strange questions or lead the interview into a discussion that may be difficult for you, just take control by phrasing the ending of any answer to any question getting them back to what's important.

21. Always follow a negative interview question with a positive answer! You can cut down your chances to be offered employment dramatically if you end questions on a negative note.

22. It's very important that you give yourself lots of encouragement and take the time out to rest during the job search process so that you can be alert, focused and confident when you get to the interview.

The Human Element

WHY DID I BEGIN JOB SEARCH COACHING?

After I graduated as a Certified Data Processor in 1996, I started helping my friends and family compose their resumes. I watched them struggle with the other aspects of their job search. I could not sit back and watch people I cared about go through so much pain during the process.

I had witnessed tears, despair, anger, confidence levels plunging down to almost nothing, hopelessness, even depression. I wanted to help. I wanted to simplify the process for them. I had taken a great course on resumes and the job search in my schooling and I started magnifying the knowledge received there by incorporating every ounce of new study and current information that I could come across. This was easy for me because it became a passion to help those in need who are otherwise going it alone. I found it personally rewarding to see others succeed and watch their confidence soar!

Let's face it- we all need a little help with our confidence sometimes!

There are some wonderful books out there regarding job searching, body language, success roadmaps, etc. so I started hitting the books to see how I could assist them even more and be able to answer some of their toughest questions as well as incorporating the best of them all into one convenient system to maximize their individual success. Since then, I have enjoyed teaching and helping people with their resumes to make these people look great on paper as well as in person! I have found a lot of fulfillment with this. There are not many times in my life when I can remember feeling happier than just walking out of my classroom and having a student tell me that I have helped them somehow. This feeling is incredibly amazing but I knew I would be investing the greatest commodity that I have, and the one thing that I truly have the least of- my TIME.

I know that if you invest your time and energy into healing others, you in turn will be healed as well. Focus on your gifts that you were naturally given. They are not talents that you should hoard for yourself; they are gifts to the world through you and your amazing personal influence. This is one of my passions. I am fulfilling my inner truth, I hope you do as well and you are the only person who can recognize what that truth is within yourself. I really hope you have fun with this course and allow yourself to find inner peace at your place of employment! Now that you know a little about me, let's address an issue that I feel has been so very damaging to so many people at the time in their lives when they are struggling to put food on the table, corrosion of confidence.

Corrosion of Confidence:

Factors of this terrible deterrent to success come from many places, some are from a variety of pressures as well as unfairness, communication errors, anger, drained energy, self-demeaning thoughts, health issues, lack of proper rest, depression etc.

Depression and corrosion of confidence is very real

It can be absolutely debilitating. Please try not to allow yourself to stay in bed due to any of these factors of corrosion. (Although I know all too well that the first thing you might want to do is throw the covers over your face and forget what your daily challenges are!) Please don't do this to yourself! I have known many people face these same challenges and have gone through similar feelings and I want you to know that you are certainly not alone and I also want you to know that you have the power to heal yourself!

Rest your body and your mind!

You will need your rest during the employment search process. When we are rested, we not only feel better, but we are truly stronger to face all of the different aspects of the job search which can be a true struggle sometimes. When we are well rested, our eyes are clearer and whiter and more beautiful, as well as we won't have those telling bags under our eyes that we seem to acquire from allowing ourselves to become overworked and overstressed. Our minds are also much clearer and focused when we are full of energy. It is also mood enhancing due to our energy levels being recuperated.

Don't deplete your energy reserves

The key is to make sure that you are spending the time and effort needed to dedicate to your job search while taking care of yourself at the same time. A good example is to make sure that you are conducting your search during the regular business hours that you would normally be working once you get the job and not at other times. That way you are not depleting your energy reserves. You are not going to look well or feel well when you show up for an early morning interview when you have been up all night searching for jobs on the internet!

Maintain your physical and mental well being

Consider the time that you search as your regular job until you get the one you want and then after your four job search hours of the day are done, go back to your family, your friends, whatever you do on your spare time normally and have fun and rest, just like you would do when you have a regular job. It is very important to keep your physical and mental health strong during your search.

You will need your strength, so make sure that you are taking care of YOU first!

PAINFUL PAST WORK EXPERIENCES

WHAT ABOUT THE HUMAN ELEMENT?

First things first! Before we move on further to all of the tips and tricks, I know that the job search can take a large toll on our self-esteem, our pocket book and our overall stress level so before we start, please make sure that you read this next part and really take it all in! There are tons of fancy books out there on the interview process but I have been incredibly surprised that these same books never touch on the human element and the stress level that you may be experiencing at this time in your life.

Quick Tip!

Searching for employment does not carry the same stigma that it has in the past. It is now widely accepted that the average person changes jobs every five years.

High stress levels can slow you down to a halt!

I haven't had one student that has not gone through some level of stress during their job search. This is normal and sadly I see it in many of my students' experiences. I spend a lot of time counseling with them on their emotional well-being because that is actually more important in my opinion than any other aspect of the job search because your stress level can slow you down to a halt. That is why I want to give you some self-assurance before we move further with the course.

LET'S BEGIN TO HEAL

What are you saying to yourself every morning?

Humility or corrosive hurt?

Having humility is good– even noble. However, beating ourselves up mentally is not a form of humility, and it is actually tearing away at the potential of all that you have to offer. You may have some emotional hurt from being let go from a job, or you may currently be in a work setting where you feel disrespected. These hurtful feelings are very real but I want you to let go of them because I want you to be able to move on and be open to new opportunities for success! The next job may open opportunities for you that are so great that a few months down the road you might wonder why you cared so much about your previous position and why you ever held onto that corrosive hurt for so long. These feelings are very real and not easily let go, especially if you have been judged by another individual or group. Maybe you were told you were not right for the company, not good enough, didn't fit in well, etc. These can all be strong weights that we carry unnecessarily.

What if I was fired?

If you have been fired for doing something that you should not have done, then please really try to visualize and understand the situation from all perspectives, learn from it, correct the behavior and move on with life. If it was something that you feel was a wrong judgment on someone else's part, try to see it from their perspective and change what you can and then move on. You will succeed but I want to make sure that you are healthy within your own thoughts about yourself before you go out there to new interviews carrying those unnecessary weights with you. Let them go, what you feel are the opinions of others and are usually just one person's opinion and do not validate the whole of who you are. They also do not necessarily represent what anyone else thinks of you personally or what anyone else thinks of your work ethic. It is your own opinion about yourself that is the most important to your future success.

ALLOW YOURSELF TO GRIEVE!

When you lose a job the grieving process can be very hard to deal with. To make it worse, you are also worried about your financial responsibilities. Honor your grief! Give yourself time to deal with your grief in order to get through the process sooner. If you are feeling shock, denial, sadness, anger, guilt, remorse, reflection and loneliness, allow yourself the time to process these emotions. Then you will be able to move forward with hope and new found acceptance. The conviction you will have at that point will be much more lucrative when job searching if you have allowed yourself to grieve and then accept what has been, what is now, and what is waiting in the future for you!

Feeling and having these emotions is very normal during a loss of any kind and if you feel you need professional help please seek it before returning to your job search. We feel the pain but then experience the new hope! As you experience these emotions remember that this time will pass! You must honor it in order to be able to get on with your job search. You can't find another job if you're still angry about the former position. You must be able to allow yourself to focus on the positive to be able to move forward with the next opportunity!

TRY TO FOCUS ON THE NEW OPPORTUNITIES AVAILABLE TO YOU!

Allow yourself to heal

People sometimes tend to dwell on the one negative when these painful experiences happen to us, and it slows them down, forgetting all of the positive experiences and compliments that have helped us move forward in our lives. These weights literally can stop you from your progression to success in your work, your personal relations, or in other aspects of your life. Take my advice, create a love for yourself that can only truly come from within yourself, take that love and allow it to release the weights that you are carrying and allow yourself to soar to your new position in life! There are always two sides to each story. There is always much more to an individual than one aspect or situation alone. I am asking you to allow yourself to heal.

Quick Tip!

If you have a company respond to you by saying that general response, "You are not right for our company" remember- that particular company is not right for YOU either!

BLOCKS TO ACHIEVING GOALS

Having a negative attitude
Focusing on unimportant things
Being closed minded
Wanting to be liked
Fear of taking risks
Low self esteem
Lack of trust in others
Fear of embarrassment
Fear of criticism/rejection
Lack of desire
Being too critical
Lack of action
Lack of commitment
Lack of purpose or vision
Trying to please everyone

Lack of accountability/responsibility
Lack of integrity
Value self more than others
Hopelessness
Helplessness
Overwhelming yourself
Jumping to conclusions
Self-labeling
Perfectionism
Fear of failure
Fear of success
Resentment
Low tolerance
Guilt and self-blame
Fear of change

I had a friend once say to me, "Why is a weed able to grow without much care, without even water sometimes but a flower takes great care to grow?" He likens this to the negative that we all pay too much attention to.

It is sometimes too easy to allow the negative to flourish when sometimes it takes a bit of care to keep the positive around you. It is important that we always try to balance the negative with true positives so that we don't cause more negative in our lives.

Try to turn all of those negative thoughts into positives, otherwise that can be all we dwell on and it is too easy to see the negatives when there are so many positives in our view.

Don't allow anyone to take your power from you!
No one can hold you back unless you allow them.
You can overcome anything as long as you believe in yourself!

16

Tips for helping to get rid of the blues

Remind yourself daily of your worth

You owe yourself that much to remember who you are. Out of everyone around you who can help you, you are the most effective person in helping with any struggles that you will be dealing with. Your worth to yourself is more important than your worth to anyone else who you may encounter.

Remember to take time to play!

After the hours of the day that you dedicate to your search, relax for the rest of the day and spend time with friends, family or your hobbies. This will recharge your batteries and rejuvenate yourself for the next day's search.

Lighten your load

Take your focus away from things that don't matter right now, get someone else to help you with the housework, or have someone help with the children so that you may have some alone time for your search. Anything that can help even in the slightest degree will make a big difference while you are in the transition period between jobs.

Recognize each destructive thought

If you are having thoughts that are discouraging, recognize these thoughts every time you have them. If you are aware of the discouraging thoughts each time you have them, you will then be able to turn these thoughts around every time!

Challenge every destructive thought!

Ask yourself first of all if the destructive thought is absolutely true, that right there can usually turn your way of thinking around because these thoughts are usually only fears and not reality. If they are not absolutely true, let them go. If they are absolutely true, ask yourself if you agree, ask yourself if everyone you know would agree, try to picture each positive person in your life when you ask yourself these questions. For instance, you may say to yourself: "I can't do that, I was never good at that." Now ask yourself "Why can't I?" "What makes me think I was never good at that?" "If I was never any good at it, why can't I try again?" Turn around every negative thought with simple reasoning techniques and allow yourself to succeed.

Get out into the fresh air and sunshine

Sometimes we get so depressed that we want to stay indoors and lock out the world. It's amazing what a little sunshine on your face can do for you. The fresh air works wonders as well. These have natural feel-good qualities. You can even incorporate this into your job search such as, you can make your calls outside in an environment that relaxes you such as a beautiful backyard, etc.

Make yourself a priority!

Make sure that you know that the most important person in your life is the same person, YOU! Take the time every day to take care of yourself in the morning, take care of yourself every time you have a destructive thought, take care of yourself in the evening and get plenty of sleep.

Release your stress with laughter!

Allow yourself to stop worrying about work whenever possible and give yourself a chance to appreciate life. Your children, your family/siblings, your friends, the members of your book club, anyone you can let go and laugh with will be a wonderful addition for you to be spending more time with during your job search.

Remember compliments

Take a moment to remind yourself of the most cherished compliments you have received in your life. It does not matter how long ago, or from whom, it only matters that you remember the compliment. Taking two minutes every day to actually stop and think positive thoughts can make all the difference in how you will be able to react to the day's trials. You may also want to take this a step further and write these down because when you are having a hard time it is not as easy to remember these compliments and those are precisely the times you need to remember them the most!

Ask your creator for help

Don't leave your creator out of one of the most important decisions of your life. The process will become easier if you know that you are not shouldering all of the responsibilities that you are facing alone.

Get prepared!

You are taking the first steps to get prepared by going through this course. When you are prepared to face the initial contacts, the interviews, etc. you do not need to worry anymore. You will have the knowledge to get you through the tough parts and you may even end up enjoying your search!

Do not make comparisons

Do not compare yourself with what your view is of any other person. You never know what their personal challenges are. In the same way, do not compare yourself to the person who you used to be, how much you used to be able to do that you now may not be able to, or what you think that others think of you or how you think you are measured in their eyes. Every scenario I have just listed is time wasted and would be feeding regrets and painful experiences. You can't afford to be stuck in a state of destructive comparison. It's just that- destructive!

You are what you think!

Keep your thoughts pure while working towards your goals. Use your gift of imagination to imagine yourself where you want to be. Include the visual surroundings, include the smells around you and include the wonderful feelings that come from achieving the success you desire. You will not attain what you want until you can envision and be ready for what you want first. Our minds are very powerful and you can think yourself into great success! In the same way, you can think yourself into failure as well, this it why it is so important that we keep our thoughts of ourselves positive at all times.

Accept that everything may never be perfect

This is a hard one for all the perfectionists like myself, but if we can face the fact that everything may not be perfect, our jobs, our homes, our families, ourselves, etc. we will not be let down when the inevitable happens, and our imperfection starts to show through our facade. We do need to spend some time planning on how we will conduct our search but do not spend most of the time on the plans, just make a quick plan and stick to it. The plan will never be perfect and it does not need to be. You can change it along the way. The employment opportunity that is waiting for you may be right around the corner and too much planning could slow your advancement down.

Be dependent on your own diversity and not the company you work for

Take the time in Chapter 2 to do the workshops to get to know your talents and interests. If you go to work knowing that your job is the only type of employment that you will be successful at, then the company owns you. You need to be independent of your company. Diversify yourself, keep your mind open to all possibilities, even the opportunities that may bring you less money can sometimes bring the most happiness, especially in knowing that if you are let go by the company, you will always have other options. Knowing this is incredibly valuable!

Help others succeed!

I strongly believe that through helping others you can help and heal yourself. This is a truth that can be measured every time you check how you feel after you have helped another person get through a trying time of their own. Some people can actually learn by teaching others and through helping others. An added benefit is the confidence and knowledge that you earn that comes from helping people conquer their own fears and elements of destruction.

Remember- there are things in life that have more importance than what our employment status is!

 Too often we measure ourselves by what type of employment we have. We are asked far too often the simple question, "What do you do?" This exasperates the problem of measuring ourselves by what type of employment we have or if we are working at all. Ask yourself what you want in life and you may be surprised to find that not everything you want or need revolves around your employment. Some examples are, I want to have a good relationship, I want to be a good parent, I want to have a healthy sex life, I want to keep my body strong and healthy, I want to be self-confident, I want to do more for my family members, etc. Most of our more precious goals in life have nothing to do with which type of employment we choose.

FIND YOUR BALANCE!

Remind yourself of your strengths to be more confident

Re-read the answers you will write down in the workshop in Chapter 1 often. This is the worksheet where you listed all of the things that you like about yourself. Keep this page in your data organizer. As you review things about yourself before interviews, you will also be able to review this page at the same time, and this happens to be one of the times that you may need to hear it most! Don't forget to add to it when you think of something else you find that you like about yourself!

Get Physical

You can take some of the edge off of your stress by simply exercising. Choose activities that are fun such as golfing, biking, baseball, walk in the park, etc. Exercise can do wonders for minimizing your stress level as well as boosting your confidence! Activities that you consider fun will be done much more frequently.

Personal Gifts of Encouragement

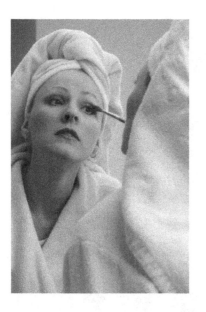

When you look in the mirror, if you are telling yourself that you are too much of something or not enough of something or if you are comparing yourself with other people's success, then you are absolutely not being fair to yourself.

Stay positive with yourself and forgive the challenges that you have because these challenges are uniquely you as well and that is part of you as a whole. Change what you can change and learn to own and love what you cannot change. All aspects are equally important to acknowledge within yourself!

Think of someone in your life who absolutely adores you! This could be your mother, your husband, your child, etc. Everyone has someone that truly admires them. Begin to view yourself just like that person who loves you the most views you. Picture that person in your mind and be them for just a moment as you look at yourself through their perspective. Pretty powerful stuff! You can see yourself with a new and refreshing perspective of your worth. Answer these questions as you do this visualization technique, and writing these answers down may help you at future times for reviewing whenever you need a lift.

- *What new qualities do you now see in yourself?*
- *Do you see why these wonderful qualities are so valuable?*
- *How does your vision change when you view yourself from their perspective?*
- *Will you now allow yourself to accept your challenges as well as accepting your individual worth?*

Workshop

Think about those questions sincerely and actually write down your answers to these questions just posed to you in the box below. You just may be amazed at the perception difference! It's too easy to let our flaws mold our perception of ourselves because we know ourselves better than anyone else, and can therefore become more critical of ourselves than anyone else would be. But here is the magic, not every new person you come into contact with knows of your previous setbacks and neither do they need to. Everyone has their own struggles, and that is how we all learn and grow.

Show future acquaintances your confidence by first showing yourself a little love today! Every day from now on, I would like you to acknowledge that you are amazing in your own unique way!

Do something to encourage and motivate yourself today!

Make it something lasting that you will see often and something that will motivate you for a long time. Give yourself a motivational note that you have to see every day. This is you, talking to you. Make it directed to yourself and how you want to feel about yourself! Place it where it grabs your attention. For instance, I have a favorite quote, "You get more with honey than with vinegar!" I learned this quote initially from my modeling and grooming and finishing teacher. I was a child back then (10-12 years old) and I always remembered my teacher's advice. I now keep this quote in my home office. It helps me remember to be kind to others and also to try to be kind to myself.

I also have two antique keys that I keep on my desk in my home office that were given to me by my son for Mother's Day and I keep those next to a beautiful butterfly that my daughter made for me for Mother's Day as well. These are placed there to remind myself that my sweet children are always with me, supporting me. This helps me when work becomes especially difficult and I enjoy the change in my frame of mind and healing when I have these precious items in view.

I have many friends who place notes with wonderful positive statements on them where they will see them every day such as: "You look fabulous!" "What a man!" etc. I also have friends who like myself, struggle with painful and debilitating diseases of the body who place encouraging statements of healing around them. They have these around them in their work environment as well as their home environment. Some notes say, "I am feeling great today!" or "My body is healing," and so on.

It sounds a bit silly but I also have a cute little fun Betty Boop sticker on my bathroom mirror which reminds me to always try to own my own inner & outer beauty because I believe a lot of people are perfectionists like me, and beat themselves up when we ultimately are imperfect. I also recognize that sticker as fun, which is another aspect of myself that I like and choose to own and enjoy because I also see the value in just having fun! I also have to smile when I see it and smiles and laughter are incredible for calming you down and helping you relax.

For the same reasons, I have always believed that every woman should have a picture of herself in her home that she views as her most beautiful self. Every woman on this planet should allow herself to own her own beauty as she is, not how the media portrays we should look. These are examples of some of the daily gifts that you can give yourself to decrease the corrosion of your confidence and in place of that create a confident, blossoming you!

These examples also show you that these reminders you give yourself can be just about anything that you want to gift to yourself to allow you more confidence & self-motivation.

No one else has to even know what they really represent because these are your private gifts that you gift yourself!

I also have a beautiful quote that most of you may recognize and I have this written on a colored piece of cardstock paper and kept in the front of my work binder above all other papers. I strategically place this page on top of all my paperwork so that I have to see it as well as physically remove it every day just to be able to get to all of my other papers and it says only this: "Life, liberty, and the pursuit of happiness!" When I am done for the day and place my papers back into the binder for the night, I place this page right back on top. That's my truth. I keep these things where I must see them with little or no effort on my part; they are in my vision at all times. We need to keep the positive around us to combat the negative. Surround yourself with things that are motivating and bring you inner joy.

I have a story about a sweet sister of mine that I would like to share with you that means a lot to me, it's a story about these small gifts of human encouragement. I had a loving sister Lori, who didn't have a lot of money but gave me a few gifts when I almost died from a near fatal kidney infection. These are gifts that she said she was embarrassed to give me as they were not expensive but I can tell you truthfully that they meant more to me than all the other gifts I had received. She gave me a cute little tough looking toy truck with big, tough looking wheels, and she laughed and said, "I don't know why I gave you this!" I was a grown woman so it was kind of funny but I immediately recognized it as a reminder of my strength, the strength that I did not feel I had at that time because I was very ill and on bed rest by orders from my doctor and being in such a fragile state, I had all but completely forgotten about how strong my body and my will truly were but that little tough looking toy truck gave me hope and reminded me that I would again someday have my physical strength back.

She also gave me a little angel because our last name is Angell but I immediately recognized that little angel as my reminder that I am being watched over through my trials and that even if I did not survive, my life was in God's hands. That thought gave me the peace and comfort that I needed to get through the struggle no matter the outcome.

Then she gave me this little crazy sounding thing I cannot hardly even describe, it was just the inside of a pet cats toy and when you shook it, it made such a crazy sound that you had no choice but to laugh every time! I have always been able to laugh through my life's challenges, but at that time in my life I certainly was missing laughter and fun and I was losing hope fast. Everything I was dealing with was very serious as I was literally facing my own mortality. Every time I shook that crazy little thing it lifted my spirits and helped me to remember to laugh. Remembering to enjoy a bit of laughter helped me relax and enjoy life as much as I could with the limitations that I had at the time.

She gave me many more little gifts that were not expensive but they were worth so much to me as I found meaning in them that gave me so much needed hope! I kept them out where I could see them constantly as I struggled to get well. I still have some of these gifts as a reminder of the gift of human encouragement that my sister and others gave me when I needed it most! She also gave me one of the greatest gifts she could, she gave me her time!

My sweet little daughter Katherine also would fill up my flower vase with flowers from my garden that I missed because I could not go outside, they were beautiful and encouraging. These gifts are the kind of gifts that speak to our souls and heal us with love. I hope that I have been able to gift you a little encouragement before you go through your search and given you some renewed energy and hope. I am continually touched by the stories and feedback that I receive from my students and I welcome you to share your stories of encouragement with me and with others around you!

These encouraging gifts such as our motivational statements that we give ourselves do not waste our money or our time at all, so please take a moment and do something similar for yourself now. Whatever works to bring your positive to you, do it and start the habit of always keeping the positive near you!

Workshop!

Write in this box what you gave yourself to promote self-encouragement.

Another one of my favorite hints for taking care of ourselves and keeping motivated is to learn to accept the compliments you receive graciously as you are deserving of each one and learn to just simply say "thank you," rather than cutting ourselves up to counteract for the compliment. This is not humility- this is just simply beating yourself up again. This is a raging, destructive form of self-depravation.

Kick that habit! Remember who you are, you are unique and you have a place. Look around you, we can learn from the confidence and happiness of the sweet children in our lives. I love watching them! Take pride in yourself, there's no one else exactly like you!

Workshop!

Write down the things that you truly like about yourself in your personal life. This can be anything from "I am funny," to "I like my ears!"

I want you to fill up this box! I know you can do it!

Chapter 2

What do I want?

This next exercise is one of the most important in my course as you will start to understand what you need in a job individually so that once you receive the job you want, you will continue to be happy with your employment for years to come!

THE KEY TO YOUR SUCCESS IS WITHIN YOU!

Use this exercise to help you decide what type of employment that your inner truth is telling you to go for!

When I create resumes for people I always tell them to do this next exercise that I have designed to get more of what they want out of life and work. First they need to know what they want and what makes them happy naturally. I have no doubt that you will get the job once you finish this course- so just make sure to accept the job that will make **YOU** as happy as possible! (Always apply for a job with the next five years in mind at least! Employers are looking for stability) You are an individual with many diverse and beautiful qualities and you may find after doing this exercise that you are qualified for more of a variety of employment opportunities that would fit closely to your personality and what would make you truly happier than you ever dreamed possible!

In two separate columns:

Write down hobbies and things you love and enjoy participating in outside work hours in the first column:

We want to make the perfect match for you and give you ideas on fields you could consider that you may not have ever thought of! This allows you to not only expand your mind but allow you to have secondary employment goals as well.

It should look something like this:

Hobbies and personal interests	*Jobs/careers that may pertain to my interests*

For instance:

If you like Music - Used CD Store, retail music store, stores where you hear music while at work, (such as a mall store or a laid back company), restaurants like Hard Rock Café, retail instrument shop, instrument repair shop, concert hall, intern position to get your foot in the door of a recording company, and so on.

- *Get Specific*! – Now list specific company names such as: Second spin CD's, FYE (For your entertainment), Afterthoughts, numerous clothing stores, Hard Rock Café, The Music Store, Holladay music, Katherine's Violins, Abravanel Hall, etc.

If you like Animals - Volunteer for animal shelter, full time animal shelter work, part time shelter work, small retail pet store, larger retail pet store, animal clinic, animal training, local zoo, internship with a veterinarian, grooming shop, boarding shop, etc.

- *Get Specific*! – Your County Animal Shelter, The Humane Society, Marks Ark, Petco, Petsmart, Brickyard Animal Hospital, Dog Bakery, The Living Planet Aquarium, Sea World, Hogle Zoo, etc.

- *Get Specific*! With listing other types of jobs that you may have only thought of once or twice but now that you are more open can become a possibility in your life. - Tuxedo store, Flower store, Hotel, Airlines, etc.

These types of jobs and volunteer work that involve some of your natural interests tend to be the best jobs for you as you will be happier working them. You may as well put a little forethought into how you will be spending those long hours every day!

Quick Tip!

Ask yourself a quick question: What kind of books would you choose to read if you had the opportunity? This can help you figure out what subjects are of interest to you! What would you like to learn more about? What fascinates you? Now take this information and see what types of work environments might be able to incorporate your particular interests!

Workshop!

Now let's take a moment and review what we have come up with and then answer these questions:

1. Write down what jobs you have had in the past that you liked the most!

(Consider paid work, volunteer work, internship, military, etc.)

2. *Now figure out and write down why those jobs stood out to you!*

(Even if you only liked a part of your job, list the part you liked.)

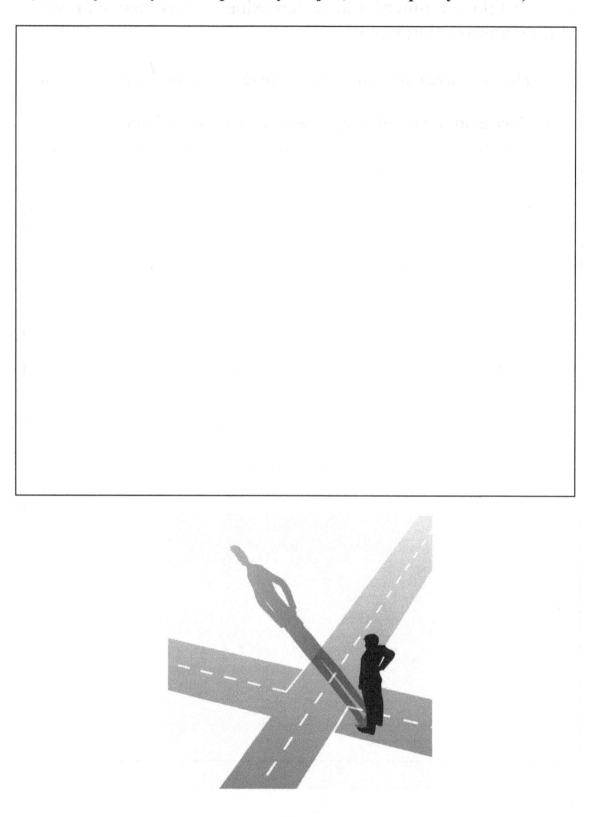

3. *Write down what jobs you disliked and what particular aspect you did not like about them.*

4. Write down what fields that you think you would have natural abilities and talents in.

(Write them down even if they require a lot of schooling as you may someday want to pursue a career in that particular field.)

5. Now, in writing, describe in detail your ultimate dream job.

The combined qualifiers for the dream jobs may not be found all at one job but you can write them down for now and narrow your job search to fit your criteria for the time being and then if your job search is becoming scarce, you can become more open to other possibilities.

It's worth a try to be the most happy you can be at your chosen position, right?

Here are some examples of dream job qualifiers:

Nighttime job, health benefits, other benefits, company with flexible hours, company that's laid back and has music playing while at work, smaller company, retail sales or a customer related job, access to the general public, company that needs artists in their line of work, morning shift, larger company, relocation, work alone, work with a team, formal environment, casual environment, etc.

Anything that you think would make you happier at work is considered a dream qualifier! Write your own personal ones here:

These may not all be attainable at the same position but you will need to know what you want, where to find it, and visualize it actually happening before you can truly *get* what you want!

6. Now write down your job criteria that you MUST HAVE in order for you to accept a position, for example:

♦ *Enough money to sustain my family and to pay my bills.*
♦ *Enough money to start or continue my savings.*
♦ *Enough work hours to sustain my family's quality of life but not too many hours that I am working myself to death.*
♦ *Enough time off for my other interests, such as my volunteering interests and regular hobbies.*
♦ *Bosses and co-workers who appreciate me for the most part.*
♦ *A job that I enjoy that I like to go to every day for the most part.*

I cannot tell you who you are, what your talents are, what your capabilities are or what will make you happy in your next job, but these exercises can help you to know what is right for you. Your decision making process should include considering all kinds of new employment opportunities and asking yourself key questions such as:

Can you see yourself carrying out all the different duties of the job?
Would you be happy doing those tasks?
Can you use your natural abilities in that job?
Does this career satisfy your basic needs?

Will I be happy working this job?

All jobs have their ups and downs and good and bad days but generally you can be honest with yourself as to the type of employment you would like to avoid all together and focus more on which jobs will compliment better with your individual personality. (This also, by pure default makes you a better visual match for your potential employer!) Remember, you will have to work the job that you choose to accept for at least the next five years!

Will this job bring me enough income to support my budget?

You may be happier at one type of job but have the background and skills for another type of job which may bring you more income. I recommend always being happy in your chosen field as you will have to be the one to actually work the job for several years but in this case, if you come across an income variance that may be a very large difference, you must decide which would be the right match for you after weighing all your options!

Am I qualified for this position?

This question is always a hard one and makes many job seekers nervous. With a little research you can know if you are qualified or not and easily say "yes" or "no" to a potential lead. If you are not qualified, do not get discouraged, at least you don't have to waste any more of your valuable time on that lead. Just move on to the next potential opportunity! Most companies will list the qualifications and if you do not understand some of the abbreviations for that particular job, you are most probably not qualified, no problem, onto the next lead!

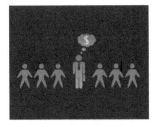

After reading this chapter, you should now have a set of target jobs that meet your work criteria- as well as been able to have a better picture of what things naturally motivate you. Now go for what you really want!

Chapter 3

Applications

Applications are especially important as some companies may review this even before they see your fabulous resume!

Less than two minutes to the "Yes" or "No" pile!

There are a few things that employers look for when weeding out many applications or resumes for the "Yes" or "No" pile in only a few moments due to time constraints. (Especially when they are working overtime to get a position filled) They do not have time to waste reading through every one of them. Eligibility, availability, salary and experience are some of the main points they initially look at. Usually you have two minutes but remember that some companies only invest 30 seconds for the overview of applications! That is how important it is to understand and answer the questions to your best advantage. Once you're in the "No" pile, expect to stay there! That means no phone call- period.

There are a few main questions that an employer has when they take an initial look at your application to quickly decide if your application is eligible for further review. These important questions are:

Legal questions:
- Legal to work in U.S.
- Over legal working age
- Felonies

Qualification questions:
- Schooling/certification
- Hours of availability
- Experience
- Salary required

Due to the time constraints on managers who are looking to fill a position, there must be good cause to keep their interest!

Open or negotiable!

On the application there are two very important fields where you need to give the interviewer as much flexibility as your personal circumstances will allow as this can give you a major edge!

The hours of availability field:

You will be in the "No" pile within moments if you do not fit their particular need at that time, which would be the time frame that they need to fill at that moment- and they do not regularly go back through the no pile to check your application again when another opening becomes available with different hours as they are looking through more current resumes when that time comes. Again, once you're in the "No" pile- expect to stay there! If you can conceivably work either the first shift or the second shift- by all means, let them know! You can place the word "Open" in that field or more preferably, you can place the exact hours that you are available such as 7:00 a.m.- 9:00 p.m. This particular time frame may get you looked at a little closer as you are more flexible with your hours. They have a time frame that they need filled in mind already before they have even looked at your application. If you want that particular job- your goal is to make it the best fit possible!

The salary field

I recommend always placing the word "Open" or the word "Negotiable" for this field. When you place an amount in that field that happens to be too high for what they can afford, you will not be contacted ("No" pile) When you place a number in that field that is too low, you may get hired, but if they give you that lower amount- you are not being paid your worth and not being offered what they may have intended to offer you in the first place. This will make a big difference every paycheck.

Do not ask about salary when picking up an application

Most companies do not allow their managers to tell the applicant what the salary range is for that particular position before the interview so it may be hard to check that figure before that time. The reason they do this is because salary is usually based on individual qualifications. The interview is the appropriate place to discuss your qualifications and what your worth is to the company in terms of salary.

Salary Negotiations

Throw the ball back in their court!

Whenever you are asked questions regarding salary during an interview setting, it can be a bit intimidating. Give yourself a break and always throw the ball back into their court by being "Open to negotiation" at all times.

You may want to ask them:
> *What do you feel that my qualifications are worth?*
> *What do you normally pay for this position?*
> *What does your budget allow for this type of position?*

<u>*Quick Tip!*</u>

Use these questions especially when questions regarding salary particulars are presented to you and you don't know what they normally offer qualified applicants. You may also simply choose to say that you are open to negotiation. In each of these instances, the interviewer is then obliged to give you an unintended "offer" and that is a good emotional trick as well as letting you know if the salary being offered is acceptable to you!

Remember, the salary being initially offered is usually a starting one and you can receive pay raises as you prove your individual worth on the job. There is nothing wrong with being silent for a moment of consideration when offered a specific salary.

Don't let salary call all the shots for you

Sometimes it is much better for you in the long run financially to accept a slight pay cut in the beginning to get your foot into a company that will allow you to advance and eventually earn more than you would somewhere else. For future success, you should be planning for a future career, not just a job that pays well.

Show your appreciation!

Always show your gratitude when an agreement is made regarding salary. Reinstate how excited you are about working for the company!

Read the directions

Yep, your grade school teacher was right! Before filling out the application, take the time to read the directions and look over the document. This can save you some serious embarrassment later! There are usually places where it states "For office use only" etc.

Be neat

Take the time to write neatly. This visual may be the first thing the employer will see about you and it is always important to the employer to have someone who prints clearly.

Fill it out completely

Do not leave sections blank. It is appropriate if the section does not apply to you to place N/A. (Non applicable)

Always be honest!

Even if you feel it would be better for you not to be honest, my advice to my students has always been to just be honest! This may be cause for dismissal if you provide false information on the application.

Compiling your data

Compiling this information is vital for the job search!

<u>*Quick Tip!*</u>

Your notebook containing your organized data will allow you to be able to have all of your information at hand within one place and you will be able to fill out an employment application in record time!

HOW TO USE YOUR DATA ORGANIZER

Your data organizer is your personal memory aid, a source you can check for complete and accurate information throughout your job search. It has room for you to insert information regarding your education, work history, skills, personal references and interview statements. Fill it out, printing it as neatly and as clearly as you would any official employment document. Once your data organizer is complete, carry it with you whenever you call on a potential employer. Use it to:

- *Organize all of the personal data you collect or develop for your job search.*
- *Provide the information you need to fill out any job application.*
- *Refresh your memory regarding your work accomplishments prior to interview appointments!*
- *Refresh your memory about your transferable skills and your best answers to interview questions.*

These next few pages mirror questions that you will need to answer when filling out applications. You can create your own notebook yourself for compiling your data or you're welcome to use the pages supplied. It will need to look something like these next few pages with the complete information included for each section:

FILL EACH SECTION OUT COMPLETELY!

PERSONAL IDENTIFICATION

Name

_____

Social Security Number _____ - _____ - _____

Present Address

_____

_____

Move in date _____
Time at current address _____ years _____ months

(List addresses for the past 10 years)

Previous address

_____

_____

Move in date _____ Move out date _____
Time at previous address _____ years _____ months

Previous address

_____

_____

Move in date _____ Move out date _____
Time at previous address _____ years _____ months

Previous address

_____

_____

Move in date _____ Move out date _____
Time at previous address _____ years _____ months

Permanent address (If different from your present address)

_____

_____

Telephone-- Home (_____) _____
                Other (_____) _____
                Work (_____) _____

Driver's License Number _____
Type_____
State issued _____ Expiration date _____
If you are not a U.S. citizen, you will need to have your visa number handy as well:
Visa Number _____ Type _____

Make sure that you provide proof of Identification/Eligibility to work. Here are some examples of forms you may need to include with your personal work portfolio:

Passport
Certificate of U.S. Citizenship
Certificate of Naturalization
Alien Registration Card
Temporary Resident Card
Employment Authorization Card
INS Reentry Permit
Refugee Travel Document
INS Employment Authorization Document

U.S. Military Identification Card
Government Identification Card with Photo
School Identification Card with Photo
Voter Registration Card
Native American Tribal Document
Social Security Card
Birth Certificate
Citizen Identification Card
Driver's License

Information for your emergency contact:

Name
_____

Relationship
_____

Address
_____
_____

Telephone-- Home (_____) _____
          Work (_____) _____ Ext _____
          Cell (_____) _____

PROFESSIONAL REFERENCES

There are four different types of references; employment, professional, academic and personal. Work and professional references usually carry the most weight. However, academic references can be very powerful as well.

Reference #1
Name _____
Address _____
City, State, Zip _____
Telephone   Home (____) _____ Work (____) _____ ext _____
    Length of time known _____ Relationship _____
Occupation _____ Company _____
Best time of day to contact this reference: _____

Reference #2
 Name _____
Address _____
City, State, Zip _____
Telephone   Home (____) _____ Work (____) _____ ext _____
    Length of time known _____ Relationship _____
Occupation _____ Company _____
Best time of day to contact this reference: _____

Reference #3
Name _____
Address _____
City, State, Zip _____
Telephone   Home (____) _____ Work (____) _____ ext _____
    Length of time known _____ Relationship _____
Occupation _____ Company _____
Best time of day to contact this reference: _____

PERSONAL REFERENCES

Reference #1
Name _____

Address _____

City, State, Zip _____

Telephone   Home (____) _____ Work (____) _____ ext _____

      Length of time known _____ Relationship _____

Occupation _____ Company _____

Best time of day to contact this reference: _____

Reference #2
Name _____

Address _____

City, State, Zip _____

Telephone   Home (____) _____ Work (____) _____ ext _____

      Length of time known _____ Relationship _____

Occupation _____ Company _____

Best time of day to contact this reference: _____

Reference #3
Name _____

Address _____

City, State, Zip _____

Telephone   Home (____) _____ Work (____) _____ ext _____

      Length of time known _____ Relationship _____

Occupation _____ Company _____

Best time of day to contact this reference: _____

JOB-RELATED INFORMATION

Make sure that you make the decision regarding each question that is best for your lifestyle before you fill out any application!

Position Desired _____

(Second Choice) _____

Salary Desired _____ Date available for work _____

Preferred Hours: Sun   Mon   Tue   Wed   Thurs   Fri   Sat

From: _____   _____   _____   _____   _____   _____   _____

To: _____   _____   _____   _____   _____   _____   _____

Are you willing to work holidays?   □ yes   Are you willing to work overtime?   □ yes

                      □ no   □ no

Are you willing to commute?   □ yes   □ no   if yes, list how far you would be willing to commute daily _____ miles

Are you willing to relocate?   □ yes   □ no   if yes, list any preferred locations below

_____

_____

List any professional organizations you are affiliated with:

Name of organization _____

Office _____

Name of organization _____

Office _____

Additional language: (Write, read, converse)

_____

How the additional language was acquired: (Schooling, travel, family ties, etc.)

_____

Quick Tip!

Every experience you have had in your work, volunteer and even your personal life has molded you into the individual that you are today. Each experience, whether positive or negative has given you experience, skills and perspective.

There are employers out there who are looking for someone just like you to work for them and your past experience has prepared you to fulfill their future needs.

TRAINING

Make sure that you list all certificates, registrations and licenses that you have obtained. You never know what may be of interest to a prospective employer! Always include the information for the type of license you have obtained as well as the date of completion.

Fields of Study and Special Courses	Number of Hours Completed	Diploma/Degree	Grade Point Average

Name of School	Address and Phone Number	Graduation Date

WORK EXPERIENCE INFORMATION

You will fill out this type of information for each previous as well as current employer that you have. Start with your most recent employment experience.

Name of employer _____

Company Address _____

Telephone (____) _____-_____

Start Date (Month/Year) [/   ]   End Date (Month/Year) [/   ]

Starting Position _____

Ending Position _____

Starting Salary _____ Ending Salary _____

Name of Supervisor _____ Title _____

Reason for Leaving (keep it positive!)

_____

Explanation of any job gaps

_____

List your 5 major job duties. (List any supervisory duties as well)	List any other responsibilities
1. _____ 2. _____ 3. _____ 4. _____ 5. _____	_____ _____ _____ _____ _____

List any type of software. Tools, machines and general equipment used on the job	List any merit raises, promotions, awards, commendations, etc. and explain
_____ _____ _____ _____ _____ _____ _____ _____	_____ _____
	Notes: _____ _____ _____ _____

WORK EXPERIENCE INFORMATION

Name of employer _____

Company Address _____

Telephone (____) _____-_____

Start Date (Month/Year) [/]   End Date (Month/Year) [/]

Starting Position _____

Ending Position _____

Starting Salary _____ Ending Salary _____

Name of Supervisor _____ Title _____

Reason for Leaving (keep it positive!)

_____

Explanation of any job gaps

_____

List your 5 major job duties.
(List any supervisory duties as well)

1. _____
2. _____
3. _____
4. _____
5. _____

List any other responsibilities

_____
_____
_____
_____
_____

List any type of software. Tools, machines and general equipment used on the job

_____
_____
_____
_____
_____
_____
_____
_____

List any merit raises, promotions, awards, commendations, etc. and explain

_____
_____
_____

Notes: _____
_____
_____
_____

WORK EXPERIENCE INFORMATION

Name of employer _____

Company Address _____

Telephone (_____) _____-_____

Start Date (Month/Year) [/   ]   End Date (Month/Year) [/   ]

Starting Position _____

Ending Position _____

Starting Salary _____ Ending Salary _____

Name of Supervisor _____ Title _____

Reason for Leaving (keep it positive!)

_____

Explanation of any job gaps

_____

List your 5 major job duties. (List any supervisory duties as well)	List any other responsibilities
1. _____ 2. _____ 3. _____ 4. _____ 5. _____	_____ _____ _____ _____ _____

List any type of software. Tools, machines and general equipment used on the job	List any merit raises, promotions, awards, commendations, etc. and explain
_____ _____ _____ _____ _____ _____ _____ _____	_____ _____ _____
	Notes: _____ _____ _____ _____

WORK EXPERIENCE INFORMATION

Name of employer _____
Company Address _____
Telephone (____) _____-_____

Start Date (Month/Year) [/   ]   End Date (Month/Year) [/   ]

Starting Position _____
Ending Position _____
Starting Salary _____   Ending Salary _____
Name of Supervisor _____ Title _____
Reason for Leaving (keep it positive!)
_____

Explanation of any job gaps
_____

List your 5 major job duties. (List any supervisory duties as well) 1. _____ 2. _____ 3. _____ 4. _____ 5. _____	List any other responsibilities _____ _____ _____ _____ _____
List any type of software. Tools, machines and general equipment used on the job _____ _____ _____ _____ _____ _____ _____ _____	List any merit raises, promotions, awards, commendations, etc. and explain _____ _____ _____ Notes: _____ _____ _____ _____

WORK EXPERIENCE INFORMATION

Name of employer _____

Company Address _____

Telephone (____) _____-_____

Start Date (Month/Year) [/   ]   End Date (Month/Year) [/   ]

Starting Position _____

Ending Position _____

Starting Salary _____ Ending Salary _____

Name of Supervisor _____ Title _____

Reason for Leaving (keep it positive!)

_____

Explanation of any job gaps

_____

| List your 5 major job duties.
(List any supervisory duties as well)

1. _____
2. _____
3. _____
4. _____
5. _____ | List any other responsibilities

_____
_____
_____
_____
_____
_____ |
| List any type of software. Tools, machines and general equipment used on the job

_____
_____
_____
_____
_____
_____
_____ | List any merit raises, promotions, awards, commendations, etc. and explain

_____
_____
_____

Notes: _____
_____
_____
_____ |

VOLUNTEER EXPERIENCE INFORMATION

You will fill out this type of information for each previous as well as current employer that you have. Start with your most recent employment experience.

Name of employer _____

Company Address _____

Telephone (____) _____-_____

Start Date (Month/Year) [/   ]   End Date (Month/Year) [/   ]

Starting Position _____

Ending Position _____

Starting Salary _____   Ending Salary _____

Name of Supervisor _____   Title _____

Reason for Leaving (keep it positive!)

_____

Explanation of any job gaps

_____

List your 5 major job duties. (List any supervisory duties as well)	List any other responsibilities
1. _____ 2. _____ 3. _____ 4. _____ 5. _____	_____ _____ _____ _____ _____ _____

List any type of software. Tools, machines and general equipment used on the job	List any merit raises, promotions, awards, commendations, etc. and explain
_____ _____ _____ _____ _____ _____ _____	_____ _____
	Notes: _____ _____ _____

VOLUNTEER EXPERIENCE INFORMATION

You will fill out this type of information for each previous as well as current employer that you have. Start with your most recent employment experience.

Name of employer _____

Company Address _____

Telephone (_____) _____-_____

Start Date (Month/Year) [/   ]   End Date (Month/Year) [/   ]

Starting Position _____

Ending Position _____

Starting Salary _____ Ending Salary _____

Name of Supervisor _____ Title _____

Reason for Leaving (keep it positive!)

_____

Explanation of any job gaps

_____

List your 5 major job duties. (List any supervisory duties as well)	List any other responsibilities
1. _____ 2. _____ 3. _____ 4. _____ 5. _____	_____ _____ _____ _____ _____

List any type of software. Tools, machines and general equipment used on the job	List any merit raises, promotions, awards, commendations, etc. and explain
_____ _____ _____ _____ _____ _____ _____ _____	_____ _____
	Notes: _____ _____ _____ _____

MILITARY EXPERIENCE

Service Branch _____ From _____ To _____
Highest Rank Held _____ Service Number _____
Armed Force Code _____ Honorable Discharge? □ yes □ no

Explanation of any job gaps
_____

List your 5 major job duties. (List any supervisory duties as well) 1. _____ 2. _____ 3. _____ 4. _____ 5. _____	List any other responsibilities _____ _____ _____ _____ _____ _____
List any type of software. Tools, machines and general equipment used on the job _____ _____ _____ _____ _____ _____ _____ _____ _____	List any merit raises, promotions, awards, commendations, etc. and explain _____ _____ Notes: _____ _____ _____ _____

QUESTIONS TO ASK EMPLOYERS DURING AN INTERVIEW

1. _____
   _____

2. _____
   _____

3. _____
   _____

4. _____
   _____

5. _____
   _____

You may choose from the many example questions in the interview chapter or come up with some of your own.

Review the information contained in your data organizer regularly!

Review the information that you compile in your data organizer as well as your key descriptive words that you have chosen before you attend each interview. You may also write down special achievement information about that particular job that you are proud of. Use these statements in the interview and really believe them about yourself!

Spend time initially to save time later

Spending a little time compiling your employment data initially saves LOTS of your precious time later! I cannot stress this enough, take a few hours if you have to- but fill out your data organizer completely! You only have to do this once and it is well worth the time you spend creating it. This is much better than trying to find all of this information over and over, every time you fill out an application! Use this to your advantage- you will have your info at your fingertips at all times! It's a no-brainer!

Keep It Current

When you are done compiling your information, you also need to keep it current. This will help you feel confident that you are always prepared when you need it!

Sample game plan:

You have to have some sort of game plan for your job search. Here is an example game plan, use it as a guide, yours may look slightly different but try to use your game plan to get organized and give yourself confidence to move forward with your search.

- ☐ Finish the worksheets in chapter 2 so I know what I want and where to go during my job search.
- ☐ Fill out or place on a separate notepad all of the items in chapter 3 for my data organizer so I am ready to fill out applications.
- ☐ Familiarize myself with all of the tips and tricks for all aspects of the search so I can make the best of each connection I make with employers.
- ☐ Compose and complete my resume so that I am prepared to pass it out during my search.
- ☐ Make extra copies of my resume and keep them in a folder that I will take to each interview and to fill out applications.
- ☐ Place my finished data organizer in this folder so everything is where I will need it for applications and interviews.
- ☐ Place a few pens and a pencil with a large pad of paper in this folder as well.
- ☐ Go through my closet and locate the best clothes for interviews and for wearing when at the future position.
- ☐ Check to make sure all items are ready to wear. (Clean shoes, tailor pants, mend buttons, iron jackets, get dry cleaning done etc.)
- ☐ Purchase staple garments and any items that I may need for my future job so that I am ready to accept a position when offered.
- ☐ Buy mints to take with me for the first contact, interview and to always have with me at work.
- ☐ Have at least 2 practice interviews with friends or family members.
- ☐ Encourage feedback from my practice interviewers, (Things they have noticed you have done well and also things you will need to work on) so that I can work on showing my strengths and work on any struggles I might have with questioning. (It's also nice to have this in writing to go over)
- ☐ From finished data organizer: Review my strengths daily before each interview and practice answering regular and especially problem questions.
- ☐ Practice saying my strength statements (Interview chapter) so that every time I go to an interview I will remember them and be able to say them readily and smoothly.
- ☐ Make sure to keep my hours straight and get adequate sleep so that my body will be ready for contacts and my brain will be sharp.
- ☐ Send a thank you letter after each interview and personalize them to each specific company and interviewer.
- ☐ Go back to my answers in chapter 2 if I am having a hard time with getting a job in certain fields to give me ideas for other avenues to pursue.
- ☐ Give myself daily encouragement!
- ☐ Review Chapter 8 before and after getting the job so that I keep the job I want!

With my finished resume and data organizer:

I am dedicating 20 hours a week to my job search.
I will conduct my search between the hours of 8:00 a.m. to 12:00 p.m. every weekday. These four hours a day will be spent:
- ▪ Networking – Talking to acquaintances in person, Calling, e-mailing, faxing my friends, neighbors, etc.
- ▪ Making initial contacts with employers.
- ▪ Sending thank you notes to employers I have interviewed with.

Chapter 4

Job Search Tips

Okay, now that we have given ourselves some renewed encouragement, we are ready to get down to business with some excellent job search tips! These are the best of the best so apply them well and I am certain that you will succeed!

Making the most of your search!

Take a look at the chart below, 48% of people looking for work find work through their personal network just by talking to people through word of mouth referrals. 24% of people attain jobs through direct contact with companies, 23% through employment agencies and recruiters and 5% through answering advertisements and internet listings. Make your search match these statistics by spending most of your time networking and with direct contact with companies and limit your time searching other avenues.

➢ **48% Word-of-mouth referrals**
➢ **24% Direct contact with companies**
➢ **23% Employment agencies and recruiters**
➢ **5% Advertisements and Internet listings**

[Source: U.S. Department of Labor, 2001]

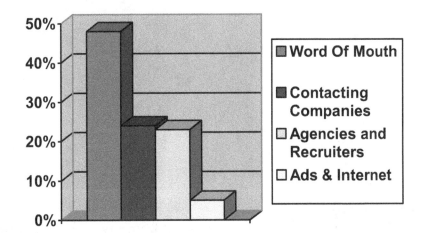

Focus most of your time on the most effective ways to job search and limit your time with the other forms of searching!

Identify a realistic job objective or career goal

You must know the type of job you want to get the maximum out of your time and efforts. Employers rarely hire people who will take just any job. You can have more than one job interest just as long as you are focused and specific with what you want generally.

Take some risks- talk with people!

Let people know you are looking for work and what types of employment you are interested in. You may want to contact friends, former acquaintances, talk with former employers, and even talk with new people you meet. Anyone can help and you never know who may be able to help you! Do not discount the help of a friend. Some companies, due to being so busy and not wanting to waste their valuable time, will first consider the applicant who was recommended by a current or former employee who they already know and respect. Utilize all sources available to you in your job search. Don't discount any opportunities that come up without investigating them further. Study the section on networking and plan this to be your first job search technique that you invest your time on. Networking is your most valuable resource!

Apply directly to the employer

Pick out the employers that interest you the most from any source available (Web listings, yellow pages, newspaper ads, etc.) and obtain their address. Appear on their doorstep at your first opportunity with resume in hand. Even if you don't know anyone there and even if you are unsure if they are hiring or not, your personal appearance can give you a big advantage if you look sharp and use your communicative skills. They will remember you when they need you!

Post your resume online

Today there are numerous resume databases on the web. Job hunters can now tap into giant online databases when launching a search prior to interviewing. Many employers today have their employment opportunities accessible through a simple phone call. The data is all there waiting for you!

Go for smaller companies

Most jobs will come from smaller companies that are growing. It is also easier to contact the important people who you will need to talk to in order to set up an interview in a smaller company.

Make more contacts!

Make a point to contact more employers each week. The average person only visits six or seven employers per month. This will only prolong your search. If you need to see 45 employers to find a job, it only makes sense to see as many employers as possible each week. Determine to see no fewer than ten employers per week at a minimum. This is only two per day minimum. Do this for as many months as your job hunt lasts. Keep going until you find the kind of employer who wants to hire you! Looking for a job is a numbers game. The more contacts you make, the more interviews you'll get. The more interviews you have, the more offers you'll get.

Quick Tip!

You can go to company internet sites for your initial contacts. Your resume can be sent via most company sites. You can get quicker responses from the company and you can also be viewed as a better candidate for using internet technology. Another added benefit is that you can research and review the company before you apply!

Work up to the job you want

Even if you have to volunteer a few hours a week of your time, getting your foot in the door may just be the ticket that you need to get started in an exciting career that fulfills your needs and allows you to utilize your talents! Leave your ego behind when you are starting at the bottom and working towards the top, it's perfectly normal and nothing to be ashamed of. We all have to start somewhere right?

Focus on your fields of interest

Try to keep your chosen jobs as in line with the field you are most interested in with a definite means to a goal for your dream job as much as possible. Your goal should be to have jobs on your resume that look like you have deliberately chosen each position and that you are moving up the ladder in a specific field. If it doesn't fit, the interviewer is wondering why you are not focused and have gone from field to field instead of sticking with one specific field and you will be asked to explain why.

Interview others

Conduct interviews of people that may have the same occupational interests as you or who may already be in the same field that you would like to be in. This is a great way to find out about the pros and cons of the occupation. It's always good to know what you are getting yourself into! This is also a great way to network because these people are already in the field and may know of someone who is hiring and be able to give you connections.

Develop your daily job search plan

Once you have narrowed your career choices, create a plan with a schedule for each of your chosen strategies and steps you will take for your daily four hour job search. Map out which activities that you plan to do each day.

This is a sample designed for job searching when laid off in mid-week. It is also designed to maximize your search by prioritizing what type of search to utilize first, second, etc. for maximum results!

Wednesday	Call everyone in your network.
Thursday	Fax resumes, phone and schedule interviews with people you were referred to from your network.
Friday	Contact companies in person that you are interested in who may not be advertising jobs at the time. Leave your resume with them.
Saturday	Rest and do whatever you would normally do on a weekend with family and friends. Recharge your batteries!
Sunday	Rest and do whatever you would normally do on a weekend with family and friends. Recharge your batteries!
Monday	Search listings from the Sunday newspaper.
Tuesday	Go to your state employment agency and review all of the current job listings and check out the specific helps that they provide for the job market in your area.
Wednesday	Research online employment listings, fax and e-mail resume.

Then you start your week over with another workable plan again until you get the job!

Stick with your plan. Your plan can be anything you want but make sure you are focused on the planned task for that day. Your job search needs to be treated as a new job and it is far easier to manage when you give it a structure and you keep a regular daily routine.

Identify your style of success!

Determine the best way to market yourself. Be yourself in your search for employment. Identify what style has brought you success in the past. Those are the skills you're most comfortable with and can use to your best advantage!

Volunteer or accept temporary work

You can be your own working advertisement by accepting a temporary position. This provides you with valuable practical experience, contacts, and references. Temporary positions are a great way for the company to see your worth! I have seen many temporary jobs turn into full time positions within the company. If they like you, they might just find a way to keep you! Volunteer for organizations and activities with business sponsors and relationships that increase your visibility and personal contacts. Explore your possibilities and leave all of your options open. You never know which method may ultimately land you your ideal job. Also, consider internships, relevant summer employment, etc.

Contact your former teachers and professors

Ask a professor or former teacher for job-leads. No one knows your capabilities, dedication, and discipline better than a teacher or professor who had the opportunity to work with you in school. Since more people find their work through direct referral by other people than by any other way, you don't want to miss making contact with them and letting them know you are searching! At the same time you talk with them about leads, you can ask them if they would be one of your personal references!

Start planning now!

If you are currently unhappy in your present position, start planning now. If you don't start now, typically your attitude will deteriorate and begin to affect your job performance- which may put your employment in jeopardy. It is more difficult mentally to conduct a job search in the later stages of this process, especially if you are fired. Although sometimes issues can be worked out with your employer, often you need to begin to explore alternatives. Prepare for your job search. Prior to starting your job search, it is crucial to learn how to prepare resumes and cover letters, complete employment applications, understand job search strategies, and practice interviewing skills.

Expand your horizons

Look for new career ideas in all areas of your life. Careers can be built on ideas from anywhere. Look for ideas in all areas of your life: at work, in traffic, shopping, or in the shower. Make brainstorming a part of your career search. Encourage others to join you in this endeavor. Use outside sources for new thoughts. Break your routines. Go to a library, museum, or city hall. Read a different newspaper or magazine. See a different kind of movie. Attend a musical event. You want new ideas and they can come from anywhere.

Research the current trends of the workforce

The better grasp you have about how global events affect the workplace, the more prepared you'll be to meet any new challenges in the future. Learn where it is going, which industries are creating new jobs and opportunities and what skills will be needed to compete in the future.

Take a personal inventory of what you want

Job hunting gives you the opportunity to go back to "square one" and review what you are all about, what skills and knowledge you have acquired, and what you want to do. Who are you? What do you want out of life? What would you enjoy in a job or career? Where are you going? Do you know how to get there? Have you been happy in your previous work? What would you like to change? What has worked for you previously and why? An inventory such as this is the best job hunting method ever devised because it focuses your view of your skills and talents as well as your inner desires. You begin your job hunt by first identifying your transferable, functional skills. By doing this you are identifying the basic building blocks of your work.

Determine what skills employers want

Find out what skills today's employers are looking for and then learn the skills that are helpful to you. If you find that you're lacking in skills that you find are necessary in your chosen field, you may be able to find resources that help you overcome that void and provide you with the knowledge and skill set that you need. For instance, if your chosen field requires you to be proficient in a certain software program for their business, you can purchase tutorial DVD's and learn to navigate through the software you need before you go for that opportunity! You may place that as one of your skills on your resume now that you have learned it! There are a variety of different kinds of training, customized training, on the job training, internships, etc.

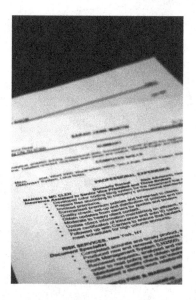

Update that resume!

A resume is what nearly everyone you approach in your job search is going to ask for. Get your resume in top shape. Keep it current to always stay prepared even if you are happy with your current employment! Use a professional service or a resume software program to prepare a fabulous, eye catching resume! You should have your paper resume finished as well as your plain text resume ready to send electronically as soon as possible! You can read more about the plain text resume in the chapter on resume sculpting.

Organize your information in a career portfolio

Prepare your data organizer sheets, your resume, your references, work samples, and other pertinent data that might be helpful during the search and interview process. Keep this information with you at every interview and each time you contact a company in person as well as via phone!

The best time to find a job is when you still have a job

To have a job already and to give two weeks' notice is very enticing to employers. That shows them that you are responsible, and they expect that you would give them the same respect of the two week notice when you leave their company as well.

Research different occupations

Find out more about the nature of the jobs that interest you, such as educational requirements, salary, working conditions, future outlook, and anything that can help you narrow your focus. Before you start meeting people, you need to know something about the industry or field you want to work in. The more you know, the better your conversations with prospective employers will be and the more impressed they will be with you and your knowledge! Also, most employers consider it a red flag if you know nothing about the job in which you are applying! Through research, you may find that particular careers are not right for you. At the same time you will know which ones you are perfect for!

Join a support group

Discouragement, all too often can come with the territory during the job search. There are many others who are facing the same challenges as you are. Being able to talk with someone is very helpful to keep your spirits up and you may even want to team up and do some brainstorming. You never know what opportunities others know about that may not be right for them but are perfect for you!

Learn from your own past work experiences

Review the last chapter called "Keeping the Job!" and ask yourself the questions under "Learn from your past work experience" designed to make you a better person as well as employee by reviewing past experiences from all perspectives.

Make cold-calls

Next to face-to-face meetings, the telephone is the most effective method available to find a job. Every call you make is an opportunity to sell yourself to a prospective employer, to pursue a new job opening, or to obtain a referral.

> ## *Quick Tip!*
>
> *Your technique with the initial telephone call can have a categorical impact on your chances to obtain what you want from the call. Make at least 10 calls per day. You will be astonished at the results! Always be agreeable, gentle, and positive. Smile when you speak! The listener will hear it. You are proving your phone as well as your people skills here! Prepare a brief outline for each call and rehearse it. Create brief statements that outline how you can help your prospective employer accomplish their goals.*

Always ask for referrals!

Any call you make to or receive from an employer may turn into a prescreened phone interview; over 50% of prospective employees are disqualified after the first phone contact is made with them by an employer. Companies do this to save time, they cannot afford to waste time interviewing every possible applicant. Remember to always be ready for a phone interview! You will usually have less than 5 minutes to make a great first impression! Here are some tips that can help you to be prepared.

Prescreened phone interview tips

- ♦ **Research the job and the company before you make the call.**
- ♦ **Figure out your role in helping this particular company with your specific skills and go over them before the call.**
- ♦ **Have your resume next to you when making the call.**
- ♦ **Turn call waiting off.**
- ♦ **Use a land line if possible to be as clear as possible.**
- ♦ **Do not chew gum or eat or drink anything on the call.**
- ♦ **Use the person's title when speaking to them.**
- ♦ **Speak slowly and listen as well when asked questions.**
- ♦ **Thank the interviewer and send a thank you note.**

Keep a script of your calls as well as a written record of what happened during each phone contact session. Here is an example format that may be helpful.

TELEPHONE CONTACTS

Date of contact: _____

Contact Person (Name and title): _____

Company Name: _____

Address: _____

Telephone Number(s): _____

Script

Introduction:

_____

Lead Statement:

_____

Body:

_____

_____

_____

Conclusion:

_____

Results/Comments:

_____

_____

Follow-up action to take:

_____

_____

We change and go through natural phases in our lives. A career that may have been right for you in your twenties may not be right for you in your forties. Don't be afraid of change! Don't be afraid to try something new, you never know what it will lead to. We are all multitalented individuals and your adaptation and acceptance of change can help you to recognize and utilize other talents that may have been previously dormant. Open your mind to possibilities you may have never dreamed of before! Let me breathe new life into you and help you find your hidden potential!

We each have so much to offer an employer. All of us have unique and wonderful qualities that are exclusive to us as individuals.

These qualities can be right for filling many different employers' needs.

Some of the most challenging times in our lives can be during the job search or when we are stuck in employment that neither fulfills us nor credits us, or is demeaning to our own truth. In these situations, I have seen many people struggle even harder to clear their minds to new possibilities when they are currently at a job that they don't enjoy because in the situation where you have no job and need employment, you usually need it immediately and are therefore forced to be open minded as it is an emergency type of situation. On the flip side, sometimes change can be even more difficult when you have someone who is very unfulfilled with their current position. I have heard phrases like, "This job is sucking the life out of me!" or "I have schooling only in this one field but I hate this field" or "I am slowly dying inside!" These people have current positions, and it is not an emergency situation to change, so they deal with their surroundings a lot longer than necessary and build more tension for their work over time.

The goal is to go to work every day at your place of employment, because you actually LIKE your job and to enjoy being around the people that you work with. I have met a woman like this. She was financially independent but she stayed at her place of employment just for the fact that she enjoyed the daily scene. She was older and also found work to be a nice change from the loneliness of being home alone all day. It seems like kind of an oddity, but it happens more often than you think, people who no longer need to work may keep at their current position much longer simply because it makes them happy to be there. Now, from an employer's perspective, how awesome would that be to have an employee who just simply enjoys coming to work every day? They don't see it as "the daily grind." They see every day as a new challenge in a field that they love. There are always going to be people and situations that are difficult to understand and deal with but truth will guide you always, your inner truth. You can start in-tuning yourself with your inner truth to find answers to any questions or struggles that you may have in life and then take that to the bank!

Here is an example of what I am talking about, let's say you have a wonderful job but you do sometimes struggle with how you were treated by a customer, etc. and at that particular point in time, you feel terrible. You don't want that situation to happen again and may feel like quitting. Ask yourself a few questions, and sometimes a good friend can do this for you as well. The questions to seeking your truth can go something like this: Logically ask yourself,

Do I really want to quit because I had one inconsiderate customer?
Do I really love my job?
Do I have bosses who respect my talents?
Do I really enjoy being around my co-workers?
Is it just the one individual co-worker making me feel like this?

When you ask yourself questions similar to these, you begin to realize your truth. Your inner truth may tell you that it is good for you at this particular time in your life to stay at your place of employment or whether it is best for you to find other opportunities at this point in your life that are more fulfilling to you.

For example, my inner truth has told me many times to stick with it in positions when it got rough at times but as I was feeling down I had to trust that I knew it was worth it because I listened to myself and what my needs were during those hard times. In contrast, I have had to leave one of my previous positions for my own better health. This was a job that I absolutely loved, I had a wonderful job with awesome co-workers, who I still hang out with today because we are great friends, and I loved every aspect of my job down to the last detail, but I was the supervisor and they worked me all three shifts within every five day work week, I'm talking day shift, then switching to graveyard and then afternoons, and never in any order.

This was truly killing me, I loved my job but when your body is constantly put through extremes like that, your body becomes ultra-fatigued and worse; your body does not know when to sleep anymore! I had to black out all of my windows in my bedroom just to be sure I could get an ounce of sleep as due to the crazy scheduling. My sleeping patterns were completely out of whack. I had to start taking sleeping pills just to get to sleep at times when my body needed to be awake. I was never truly rested. This was devastating to my body, I was always terribly fatigued. To make it worse I was dealing with a debilitating muscle disease and the stress and lack of proper sleep patterns exasperated my symptoms.

The whole staff went through similar experiences and we would let the management know about our concerns that they needed to take extra care when scheduling for individuals but they never listened and continued their erratic scheduling. Sometimes I was even scheduled for double shifts!

This company did not care to have their employees there at their 100% best, they only wanted bodies on the job, and frankly, that's what they got most of the time.

I would have employees come to me as their supervisor in tears telling me that they cannot take the way the management is never open to listen to them. I would beg them to stay because I knew the turnover rate was very high and I also knew that the scheduling was precisely why we were constantly having to hire and it made me feel helpless that this was a situation out of my control, even though I had let the management know of everyone's concerns several times.

When I first got there it took 3 months of training time for any new employee to become fully trained in the positions that I was overseeing. I cut that down to a month and a half training time but the turnover rate was still burying us alive right at the three month mark so right after someone would be finally trained on everything and we knew them, loved them and needed them, they wanted to leave due to the scheduling issues. This devastated their business.

I tell you that story because you do not have to accept anything like this in your work environment. I would accept the sad 3:00 a.m. phone calls from the desperate employees who wanted to quit because I knew if I didn't take these calls, I may not have had a staff the next day! These employers had wonderful, high quality, loyal, dedicated employees and they took advantage of them rather than appreciating them.

Some of those wonderful employees are still there and are still dying inside because of their extreme loyalty. What a shame for an employer not to realize and appreciate that!

It's too bad that these same employees aren't more loyal to themselves at that point. If you show that you are serious about your work and really want to give your employer your time and talents and even a love for your work, they should definitely take notice as that is a very valuable quality to their business. This is not a perception of value; this is true value to them. If they never do take notice of your work ethic and integrity then that is most likely not the employer that will fulfill you the most. Please keep that in mind as you decide who you will stay with and who you won't. Although I loved this job, I had to leave to stay healthy. Be true to yourself first! Your inner truth will guide you.

Keep yourself dedicated, strong, positioned, and consistent. Job hunting can certainly be one of life's most stressful experiences. You have more power to keep the pressures of job hunting under control than you may think!

The key is to focus your job search and stay strong, dedicated and consistent. One of the curious things about the human brain is that it focuses on only one thing at a time. So keep it focused on you-- and finding the job that will best satisfy your needs.

You need to give yourself the strength to do all that is needed to be able to focus full time on your job search. Don't waste your energy on projects that aren't necessary right now. Regain composure, stop beating yourself up– you cannot see clearly when you are in that mindset– because you are too busy closing your eyes and dodging the punches coming from the person that should be your very best ally--- YOURSELF!

ARE YOU NETWORKING?

Networking would be the best time investment you can make!
Most experts agree that networking is the most important job search
technique that you can spend your time on. Most say it is the only one
job search technique that really matters and that all other techniques
are in support of networking.

**Networking is that important but yet it is the technique that the
least amount of time is spent on the average job search!**

What is a network?
A network consists of all the people you know as well as all of the people they know.

What is networking?
Networking is talking to various people in your network to either get the information or to find
other people who may have the information that you want so that you will be able to speak to
employers about employment opportunities.

*Networking can get you considered sometimes before you even send in your
resume! Friends help you find work not strangers!*

Quick Tip!

*Networking can also let you know of opportunities that may not be advertised. This is
called the "hidden job market" which accounts for about 80% of all available jobs!*

How to build your network of people to contact

Make a list of people you know such as:

Relatives, friends, neighbors, volunteer groups, church groups, former employers, doctors, stockbrokers, dentists, former co-workers, former teachers, college alumni, bankers, club members, lawyers, accountants, insurance agents, etc.

This is a sample list, take into account everyone you know as well as everyone that you may see in the course of your day such as a drycleaner, a store clerk, etc.

YOU ALREADY KNOW EVERYONE YOU NEED TO KNOW!

Don't leave out ANYONE!
You never know who might know a lot of other people, or who may know something about your chosen career!

Tips to help you when contacting your network

That's all there is to it! Don't stress! Stay casual with it, these are people who you know and are already acquainted with.

1. Simply tell them that you are looking for work.
2. Let them know what types of employment that you may be interested in.
3. Give them a business card or a note with your contact information when meeting in person.
4. Ask them to please let you know if they think of someone that they know that you may be able to contact for an interview. If they let you know a name to contact, be sure to ask them if you can use his or her name when contacting that person.
5. Ask them to keep you in mind if they hear of any new opportunities that come up that may be a good match. Let them know that you appreciate them keeping you in mind.
6. Keep notes regarding each networking contact and notes of what the outcome was. Periodically look through them to see if you need to call back anyone and follow through.

This is a sheet that is helpful when you are calling network contacts!

Networking Worksheet

Name: _____   Date called _____ / _____ / _____

Company name: _____

Address: _____

Phone: _____   Appointment time/date: _____

Follow-up: _____

Summary of conversation/contact:
_____
_____
_____

Contact names received:
Name _____
Position _____
Company _____
Phone/fax _____

Contact names received:
Name _____
Position _____
Company _____
Phone/fax _____

Contact names received:
Name _____
Position _____
Company _____
Phone/fax _____

When NOT to accept the job offer!

There may be times that you will be offered a job very quickly such as with commission based employment. This seems like it might be a good thing but beware of quick job offers!

Here are some tips to help you stay on top of some of the current scams so that you don't waste your money or something even more precious- your time!

Employment Agencies

There are numerous job-hunting websites now available that post jobs for private industry. Many companies also offer a way to apply online. However, these sites do not replace traditional and proven job-hunting approaches such as networking, personal contacts, business organizations and interviewing.

During your search you may come across ads from employment agencies that promise wonderful opportunities. While some companies honestly want to help you, others can be more interested in taking your money.

BE WARY OF:

- ♦ **Promises to get you a job and a guaranteed income.**
- ♦ **Upfront fees, even if you are guaranteed a refund if you are dissatisfied.**
- ♦ **Employment agencies whose ads read like job ads.**
- ♦ **Promotions of "previously undisclosed" government jobs. All federal jobs are announced to the public at** <u>www.usajobs.gov</u>

Get a copy of the employment agency contract and review it carefully before you pay any money. Check with your local consumer protection agency and the Better Business Bureau to see if any complaints have been filed about a company. The Federal Trade Commission sues businesses that fraudulently advertise employment openings and guarantee job placement. Contact the FTC if you have a complaint.

Work at Home Companies

Not all work-at-home opportunities keep their promises. Some classic work-at-home schemes are medical billing, envelope stuffing, and assembly or craftwork. Ads for these businesses say: "Be part of one of America's fastest growing industries. Earn thousands of dollars a month from home!" Legitimate work-at-home program promoters should tell you, in writing, what's involved with the program they are selling.

Here are some questions you might ask:

- **What tasks will I have to perform? (Ask the program sponsor to list every step of the job)**
- **Will I be paid a salary or will my pay be based on commission?**
- **Who will pay me?**
- **When will I get my first paycheck?**
- **What is the total cost of the work-at-home program, including supplies, equipment and membership fees?**
- **What will I get for my money?**

The answers to these questions may help you determine whether a work-at-home program is appropriate for your circumstances, and whether it is legitimate.

Multilevel Marketing

Some multilevel marketing plans are legitimate. However, others are illegal pyramid schemes. In pyramids, commissions are based on the number of distributors recruited. Most of the product sales are made to these distributors, not to consumers in general. The underlying goods and services, which vary from vitamins to car leases, serve only to make the schemes look legitimate. Most people end up with nothing to show for their money except the expensive products or marketing materials they were pressured to buy.

If you're thinking about joining what appears to be a legitimate multilevel marketing plan, take time to learn about the plan.

- **What is the company's track record?**
- **How long has this company been in business?**
- **What products does it sell?**
- **Does it sell products to the public-at-large?**
- **Does it have evidence to back up the claims it makes about its product?**
- **Is the product competitively priced?**
- **Is it likely to appeal to a large customer base?**
- **How much does it cost to join the plan?**
- **Are minimum monthly sales required to earn a commission?**
- **Will you be required to recruit new distributors to earn your commission?**

Net-Based Business Opportunities

The Federal Trade Commission says that many internet business opportunities are scams that promise more than they can deliver. The companies lure would-be entrepreneurs with false promises of big earnings for little effort.

Some tips to finding a legitimate opportunity:

- ◆ **Consider the promotion carefully.**
- ◆ **Get earnings claims in writing.**
- ◆ **Study the business opportunity's franchise disclosure document.**
- ◆ **Interview each previous purchaser in person, preferably at the purchaser's place of business.**
- ◆ **Contact both the local consumer protection agency and Better Business Bureau where the business opportunity promoter is based and where you live to find out whether there is any record of unsolved complaints.**
- ◆ **If the business opportunity involves selling products from well-known companies, verify the relationship with the legal department of the company whose merchandise would be promoted.**
- ◆ **Consult an attorney, accountant or other business advisor before you put any money down or sign any papers.**
- ◆ **Take your time. Promoters of fraudulent business opportunities are likely to use high-pressure sales tactics to get you to buy in. If the business opportunity is legitimate, it'll still be around when you're ready to decide.**

Quick Tip!

This may be a time that some people you know who are excited about what they are currently into will be contacting you to recruit you to do the same opportunity as well, knowing that you are on your job search. Keep in mind before you spend your time and money on these endeavors that some of these opportunities promise that you can get rich quick, (which may seem enticing) but can actually end up costing you a lot of money and time and may discourage your search.

Also, many of them are business opportunities and I am all for the successes of the entrepreneur, but most people don't realize everything that it will take to start and keep their businesses running in order to become successful. If you are not ready to take on the stress and expense of a new business, you may want to pass on their offers and keep your focus for the time being! Most people aren't making tons of money on these schemes and opportunities. These opportunities that work for one person may not be right for everyone.

Tips for Job Fairs and Career Expos

Job fairs are an opportunity to meet with employers that you might not be able to meet with in any other way. It can be a great place to network as well!

♦ Make all of the preparations that you would make before any job interview, including making sure that you are well dressed and ready to express and present yourself as a top notch applicant. Review the interview section to get lots of tips to help you in this area.

♦ Bring your full career portfolio including your resume, data organizer sheets, references, etc.

♦ Make sure to have plenty of resumes handy to pass out.

♦ Bring a folder in which you can put job information and brochures.

♦ Look for upcoming job fairs by your city and state.

♦ Lines can be long so make sure that your shoes are comfortable.

Understand your skills as well as your limitations

Understand your own skills and the language the employer is using on their advertisements to explain their requirements for applicants, such as, 60 wpm, etc. If you didn't know what "60 wpm" meant, you can almost guarantee that you are not qualified to fill the position that they are looking for.

Don't waste your time or theirs on job interviews that do not go anywhere, it will only discourage you in your search. Here are some examples of what some of the more basic abbreviations mean when looking at an employment advertisement:

admin. = administrative	**mfg. = manufacturing**
adv. = advertising	**mech. = mechanic**
agcy. = agency	**mgr. = manager**
appt. = appointment	**op., or oper. = operator**
asst. = assistant	**oppty. = opportunity**
bkgd. = background	**ot. = overtime**
clk. = clerk	**perm. = permanent**
comm. = commission	**progr. = programmer**
data pro. = data processing	**PT = part time**
dir. = director	**refs. = references**
EOE = equal opportunity employer	**rel. = reliable**
eqpt. = equipment	**req. = required**
exp. = experience	**sal. = salary**
Fr. ben. = fringe benefits	**secty. = secretary**
FT = full time	**sh. = shorthand**
gd. at fig. = good at figures	**steno. = stenographer**
gen. off. = general office	**swbd. = switchboard**
hosp. = hospital	**tech. = technical**
hqtrs. = headquarters	**temp. = temporary**
Ind. = industrial	**trnee. = trainee**
lt. type = light typing	**wpm = type words per minute**

Make sure that you are confident that you can do the job from the initial review of their needs in an applicant. If you are unsure if you qualify or think that the company may train their employees on the particular position, do not set up an interview until you know for sure. These are very basic qualifications that they listed because they were vital to the particular position and if you find that you are qualified, it will be a serious confidence builder for you when you are ready for the interview!

What do I like about myself?

Include your assets that you consider to be work related as well as any personal assets because you would be surprised at what is truly transferable between the two. I want you to place an asterisk next to any quality you possess that you consider rare. Fill at least one page up with these assets! Here are some examples:

- *I am a genuinely positive person. ***
- *I give compliments freely and equally to men as well as to women. ***
- *Every compliment I give is genuine.*
- *I like making people feel better when they're sad.*
- *I like to help people to look their best through wardrobe and makeup coloring.*
- *I am encouraging when anyone struggles with self-worth. ***
- *I find the good in any situation.***
- *I am very motivational when in supervisory positions.*
- *I know my limitations in managerial positions and own that I don't like to discipline employees.*
- *I am sensitive to the needs of special children & adults with any type of handicap. ***
- *I am very articulate.*
- *I am very intelligent.*
- *I am very creative.*
- *I am very outgoing.*
- *I am self-motivated.*
- *I really try to please others.***
- *I am fun to be around.*
- *I listen to my supervisors.*
- *I am very loyal to my company.***
- *I treat my supervisors with respect.*
- *I love children, as well as the older generation, I can continue a conversation with both.***
- *I'm genuinely interested in what the older generation has to say and enjoy learning from their life experience.*
- *I am very spontaneous, even random at times.***
- *I am hospitable.*
- *I am a very good speller.*
- *I can create any type of document needed.*
- *I like to dress up every day, I try to look good at work every day from my clothes to my makeup to my hair, I always make an effort.***
- *I like being accountable to the public.***
- *I enjoy being accommodating to others.***
- *I enjoy and cheer when others succeed rather than become jealous of their successes.*
- *People don't need to worry about what they say to me, I am trustworthy and don't become unreal and uncomfortable to people when they share their secrets with me.*
- *I work until the job is done, not until I am done.***
- *I am honest with my employer.*
- *I think things through before I act.*

Anything about yourself that you considered rare, I want you to place those attributes in your data organizer because you will want to review those before an interview when you review your other employment information!

Okay, now let's begin to own our challenges as well

Next, we will be listing our personal and professional life challenges. Challenges are not always negative; they just let you know where your limitations are. Your comfort level with certain things gives you an idea of what you can work on and what you can't change. Here are some examples to get you started:

- I don't like dealing with negative people or negativity in any way.
- I don't like being told what to do.
- I don't like getting into trouble.
- I don't like to be criticized in any way.
- I care about my job way too much sometimes.
- I care about how individuals are feeling and pick up on that readily.
- I have a bit of an ego at times.
- I need attention sometimes.
- I am too nice and have a hard time with confrontation, I usually avoid it entirely, but when that final straw is placed, look out!
- I am always happy normally, and people are shocked when I show the least bit of disapproval but by that time I don't really care what they think and after always being caring it really confuses people.
- I can become sad if someone is mean to me because I don't understand why anyone would be cruel to others as I try not to be mean to anyone. I allow it to affect me too often and they usually do not know that they have hurt me because I hide it with my smile but then I avoid future dealings with them.
- I don't like uniforms, I like my individuality.
- I don't like to hear office gossip.
- I don't like to dress casual at work.
- I don't like a messy work environment.
- I have no respect for pettiness in people.
- I will leave a job too quickly if I don't feel valued because I don't see the worth.
- I like to have the leeway for creativity and not be stifled.
- I don't like to sit or stand in one place all day.
- I need fresh air sometimes.
- I like to be talked to in a respectful manner always, I cannot stand sarcasm.
- I can laugh at myself often, but I cannot stand when someone else belittles my intelligence and they immediately lose my respect at that point.
- I can't stand not having control over my own work environment.
- I am a natural leader but I am the motivating type of leader only, so I don't like to discipline or fire people.
- I don't like answering to numerous supervisors.

Write down whatever comes to your mind, it's good for you to be able to recognize it and then you can see clearly to help fix your individual challenges whenever possible.

There, that wasn't so bad was it? Your challenges also make you uniquely you. For instance, my personal challenge of getting my feelings hurt because I am too nice might just be what an employer is looking for- someone who is nicer than the average person for a position that requires someone who is naturally sweet. You may be the exact opposite and are more stern, which is perfect for other positions that need someone more stern as well.

EVEN WHAT WE CONSIDER OUR CHALLENGES MAY BE JUST WHAT THE NEW EMPLOYER IS LOOKING FOR!

If you view each of your challenges and own them, then do what you can to locate a position that fits your challenges as well as your great assets, you will definitely soar and your employer will benefit as well!

Some key reasons why people do not get hired!

- ♦ **Poor personal appearance**
- ♦ **Poor hygiene**
- ♦ **Questionable honesty**
- ♦ **Inability to connect with the interviewer**
- ♦ **Negativity, especially about past employers or coworkers**
- ♦ **Not showing any knowledge about the company where they are applying**
- ♦ **Arrogance and overly aggressive behavior**
- ♦ **Lack of enthusiasm**
- ♦ **No sense of humor**
- ♦ **Showing up late for the interview**
- ♦ **Communication issues during the meeting**
- ♦ **Lack of self confidence**
- ♦ **Inability to take responsibility for past failures**
- ♦ **Failure to express appreciation for the interviewers time**
- ♦ **Vague responses to interview questions**
- ♦ **Bad phone skills**
- ♦ **Risky interview attire**
- ♦ **Too focused on salary issues**
- ♦ **Talking too much/bad listening skills**

Employer Expectations

Picture one of the jobs that you might want to apply for and visualize yourself as the interviewer of that particular job

Write down what you would want in to see in a potential employee in your chosen field if you were the interviewer for the job you would like to obtain. Picture that person sitting before you. Here are some examples of what interviewers are looking for.

- *Someone who is well dressed*
- *Someone who is well groomed*
- *Someone with a great smile*
- *Someone with a great attitude*
- *Someone with a fun sense of humor*
- *Someone with good listening skills*
- *Someone with good communication skills with a great greeting and salutation over the phone*
- *Someone with a confident handshake and general greeting in person*
- *Someone who is honest during the interview*
- *Someone nice whom they may want to work with for a few years*
- *Someone trainable and will take direction from them*
- *Someone who is not arrogant*
- *Someone who is confident that they are the right person for the job*
- *Someone who looks the part that they have in mind*
- *Someone who has researched their company*
- *Someone with good manners*
- *Someone who is dependable and responsible*
- *Someone who has a willingness to learn*

Now you can tailor yourself to meet their expectations!

Quick Tip!

The interviewer is normally a manager working overtime until they fill the available position so they really need you to BE that perfect person for their company as well! I believe that one of the most important things you can learn from my course is that the interviewer needs you to fill the open position just as much as you need the job!

BE the right person for the job!

Chapter 5

Initial Contacts
Tips for making contacts with companies before the interview

Come prepared!

Do not ask the secretary for a phone book or a pen to fill out an application; you should have your data organizer with you which you should have already prepared to include all of the information you need. You should always have a pen and notepad at interviews and even when you're only picking up applications. If you have your completed data organizer with you, you will be able to fill out an application in less than five minutes! Very impressive!

Go alone

Do not bring a friend with you when filling out an application, a potential employer will hire you based on your own merits, not your friends. I have never met a manager that wants to hire two friends. You are there to apply for work. Besides, if your friend says something a little off color, you may as well have said it yourself, or if they are wearing something a little too inappropriate- you are remembered for it. It's not worth it. Always go alone!

Smile at everyone you see!

If you think that the secretary's opinion does not matter think again! They are usually the one who hands your application to the employer and explains a bit about you and consequently her initial assessment of you is critical! Treat everyone at all levels extremely well before and after you get the job!

Always dress appropriately

When picking up applications or when leaving a resume, always dress like you would for the interview. Look modest. You should never dress in inappropriate clothing and nothing less is acceptable than wearing at least what you would be required to wear if you obtained the position. You do not want to look like you just walked by the establishment and decided at that very minute to apply there. A bit of research about what the company expects you to wear to work before you go in to pick up the application goes a long way! Visually you will look like you fit the job description (which is your ultimate goal right?) Dress the part.

Deliver your resume in person whenever possible!

In these times where everything is digital it is sometimes necessary to fax or e-mail your resume but only fax it or e-mail it as a last resort as the resume can look much cheaper and does not look as put together in these forms.

When picking up an application, never ask about salary

Chances are the person who will be handing you the application will not be able to tell you anything about salary and are sometimes told specifically not to discuss salary by the employer as the interviewer needs to negotiate a salary that is based on individual experience. The manager may not even be able to tell you unless you are in the interview. If learning about salary is important to you before the interview, call and ask as an anonymous person, usually the advertisement that tells the details about the job will also include this information.

Get out of the way!

Do not fill out applications where regular company business takes place such as the front counter, etc. These places are where other day to day business is being handled and you will definitely be in the way! Go out to your car and come back when you have finished filling it out or take a note book with you that would be stiff enough to use to write on and still have good handwriting and fill it out while sitting in a regular chair. You can usually take a seat and fill it out in less than five minutes directly from your data organizer. I notice every time how an applicant reacts to the application process, it tells me a lot about their personality! You don't ever want to appear unaware of yourself when applying for a job.

Quick Tip!

Expect rejection to happen every once in a while- it goes with the territory. I know it's easier said than done but try not to take rejection personally. Remember, typically you should expect to receive quite a few no's until you get one yes. (Some sources say it is one yes in up to 50 no's!) This is normal so be prepared not to expect to get the job on your first interview. If you prepare for rejection, it will be easier to handle it when it happens.

You will have many different opportunities for contacting a potential employer. You can use forms such as a response letter, a cover letter, delivering your resume, the interview, follow-up letter, phone calls, thank you letter, etc.

Cover Letters

Cover letters are letters that accompany and introduce your resume. You can send a cover letter even when you're sending your resume via e-mail.

Quick Tip!

Keep your cover letters basic! No employer has time to read a novel about anyone before they've even had a chance to review their resume!

Here are some examples in a basic format that you may follow and make necessary changes as needed for your particular situation:

Quick Tip!

One way to easily create a great cover letter is to look at any employment advertisement and list the requirements necessary for the job and then list how you are qualified to meet those requirements. For instance:

Greet the contact person by name and title

- *You require someone with a BS in finance*
- *You require someone who can type at least 30 wpm*
- *You require someone who is good with the public*

- *I have a BS in finance*
- *I type 40 wpm*
- *I am excellent with the public*

This allows the hiring manager to easily see that you are the right person for their qualifications that they specified in their advertisement. Always place the requirements in the order that they listed in the ad because the way they list them is usually the order of relevance. Then let them know that your resume is included and that you will call them for an interview. Simple as that!

Example Pre-Interview Cover Letters

_____

_____
(Your address)

_____
(Date)

_____
(Name and title of the contact person)

_____
(Name of company)

_____
(Company street address)

_____
(Company city, state and zip code)

Dear Mrs./Mr./Ms. Smith:

_____

_____
This is your introduction such as: "Please accept the attached resume as application for the ____ position." "I am very impressed with…" "My experience meets your requirements," etc.

_____

_____
This is the body of your cover letter, this can be a point by point description of what you can do for the company in the order that they gave you. You may also decide to place something more general such as: "I have been interested in this company/field for some time now and I believe I am ready to make my contribution to this field." You may also want to state a skill and how this particular skill ties in with the current position, etc.

_____
This is the conclusion of your cover letter, for example: "Once again, my experience meets your requirements, I look forward to meeting with you," "I have enclosed my resume for your review," "I will be at your office at 8:00 a.m. Monday, April 10 for our appointment," etc.

Sincerely,

_____
(Your signature)

_____
(Your name typed)

October 11, 2017

Contact person's name
Company name
Business street
Business city, state and zip

This letter is in regard to your recent ad in the Tribune for the Assistant Store Manager position. I am interested in the position and I already purchase and enjoy your products.

My work background has been primarily secretarial/business customer service with office background. I have two years of college credits in graphic design/interior design and business which would be an asset to this position.

This job would give me the opportunity to combine color design course experience with my business experience which includes banking, employee work scheduling, reports, payroll, insurance, employee training, cashier and organizational skills.

Enclosed please find my resume; I look forward to hearing from you.

Sincerely,

(Signature)
Kodi Smith

My address
My city, state and zip
My area code and phone number

Quick Tip!

Try not to use first person pronouns too often like "I" "me" "my" etc. You will probably have to use some when corresponding but keep them as few as possible! You may occasionally start a sentence but never start a paragraph in the first person!

You may take any sentence such as: "I would really enjoy working for your company," and change it to "Working for your company would be a privilege," or a contact listing such as "I can be reached at (000) 000-0000" can be changed to "Phone (000) 000-0000" etc.

Thank you notes

When sending thank you notes and letters remember to:

- ➢ **State your appreciation**
- ➢ **Express your interest in the employment opportunity**
- ➢ **Give a brief restatement of your qualifications**
- ➢ **Give a final thank you**

Quick Tip!

Thank you notes are so important! I once had two applicants that I was choosing between, they both seemed to be excellent for the position and I was going back and forth between the two as to who I would eventually hire. That same day I received a quick thank you e-mail from one of the applicants. She thanked me for my time and restated that she was very interested in the position. That's how simple the e-mail was! Guess which one was hired? The one that made the extra effort of course!

EXAMPLE THANK YOU NOTE

Jan 3, 2015

Dear Mr. Richardson,

Thank you for the interview for the accountant position today. I appreciate the information you shared with me and enjoyed meeting Ms. Jones from the accounting department.

My interest in working for Stones Inc. is stronger than ever, and based on your description of the position, I know I can do a good job for you.

I will contact you by Tuesday of next week to learn of your decision. Again, thank you for your time and consideration.

Sincerely,
(Signature)
Mr. Rick Diamond

EXAMPLE THANK YOU LETTER

July 14, 2014

Contact person's name
Linens-R-Us
Business street
Business city, state and zip

To Mr. Jones:

Thank you for the opportunity to discuss the secretarial position this morning. Our conversation gave me a better understanding of Linens-R-Us and the requirements of the job. The additional information from Mark and Katherine was helpful in gaining a better perspective of the position.

My strong office and interpersonal skills will definitely make a contribution to your company. I am proficient in all the computer software packages you use and possess the customer service experience you want.

I enjoyed meeting the office staff and touring the facility. This is clearly a quality organization with an emphasis on efficiency and a dedication to teamwork. I would consider it a privilege to join your team and look forward to hearing from you.

Again, thank you for your time and consideration.

Sincerely,
(Signature)
Mr. Thomas Martin
My address
My city, state and zip
My area code and phone number

Example Follow-Up Letter

My address
My city, state and zip
July 25, 2013

Mrs. Jane Smith
The Book Store
74285 Washington Street
New York, NY 10052

Dear Mrs. Smith,

As promised, I have enclosed a copy of my resume. Please look it over within the next few days.

Your suggestions for breaking into the book business in New York have already been helpful. I called Miss Angell right after I spoke with you and she has agreed to see me. Thank you for the lead, I appreciate your help.

Thanks again for all of your support in my job search. Please call me at home if you hear of anyone who is looking for a bright and ambitious employee.

Sincerely,
(Signature)
Mike Richardson

Keep it simple!
I prefer to keep the contact documents very simple. Keep in mind that the potential employer does not have a lot of time to waste and it is better not to lose their interest by creating a longer than necessary document for review.

Chapter 6

<u>Resume Sculpting</u>

There are three basic resume formats to display your work experience in the best way possible. These formats include:

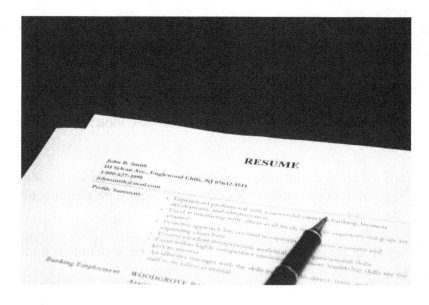

> ## Chronological

A chronological resume or CV (curriculum vitae or academic resume) shows the chronological progression of your career, from entry-level to senior-level jobs. Interviewers prefer employment with the most recent job listed first. It may also include details about where you have worked in the past, what the job duties were and dates of employment.

Pro's to using the chronological resume format:

♦ This is the format most easily recognized by most employers and also the format they want to see to easily find the information that they want to know about your history.

♦ It's a fabulous format if you have a solid career history within the same area with no major gaps in the employment history.

♦ You can showcase a steady work record with increasing responsibilities very effectively using this format.

Con's to using the chronological resume format may be:

♦ Your skills may not be as easily seen, especially at a quick glance.

♦ If you have a problem with job gaps, this format may highlight them.

♦ It is not the best format for anyone changing careers.

♦ This is not always the best format for new graduates.

♦ Work experiences over ten years old are better showcased using the functional or combination type of format.

*List the most recent job history first in the chronological order and always state the details of your most senior position first.

➢ Functional (Skills)

A functional resume or CV emphasizes your accomplishments, skills and qualifications rather than where you used or acquired them. It focuses on the skills relevant to the current job search and groups them by function or skills.

Pro's to using the functional resume format:

♦ This format is best for students, graduates, and military personnel.

♦ This is a great format for first time job seekers.

♦ This is the best format for people that have been out of the job search for long periods of time.

♦ This may also be the best format for people who are changing from one field to another.

Con's to using the functional resume format may be:

♦ In a true functional format there is no chronological listing of employment so some employers may see it as unfamiliar.

♦ It may create worry that the applicant may be trying to hide something such as; being a job hopper, lack of career progression, employment gaps, too little experience, etc.

➢ *Combination*

A combination resume or CV combines the functional and chronological formats. It lists your achievements and skills and then your job history.

Pro's to using the combination resume format:

♦ A combination format is the best choice if you have performed a diverse or unique range of job functions and you need to showcase your abilities.

♦ It is a great resume format if you have a definite career path.

♦ It is a great format if you have a targeted job that is related to your job history and experience.

*The combination resume format is very effective for many job seekers. The chronological resume can be enhanced with a section highlighting skills, accomplishments and experience. The functional resume can also be strengthened with a chronological listing of employment experiences.

Those were the three main resume formats that are most used in the job market.

Other formats include:

➢ *Inventory*

An inventory resume or CV presents a general overview of your skills, achievements and qualifications. If it states a career path or objective, it uses general terms and it should be consistent with your career goals.

Pro's to using the inventory resume format:

♦ *It's a good format if you do not have a specific employment objective.*

♦ *This type is useful if you need to compose different resumes that correspond to a different career objective.*

♦ *It's a good format if you need to send your resume to many various recruiters for the sake of time.*

Con's to using the inventory resume format may be:

- ♦ Please use caution when using the inventory format. This is not the most effective resume format.

*If you are interested in several careers, write several inventory resumes, each for a particular career goal.

➢ *Targeted*

A targeted resume or CV focuses on a particular objective within a specific industry or company. It highlights skills, qualifications and experience matching a position's requirements.

Pro's to using the targeted resume format:

- ♦ This resume format directs skills and experience to the specific needs of the employer.

- ♦ This format is most effective when you know the specifics about the position or company.

- ♦ This is a very powerful resume strategy by quickly capturing your employer's interest at a glance.

- ♦ For executive positions and specialized technical jobs, this strategy is very necessary to impress the employer.

*Using the combination format, set up a resume template with header information and the chronological summary of your employment, then customize the functional sectional of the resume, the summary of skills, accomplishments and qualifications to meet the needs of a specific employer. Be sure to word your objective with the exact job title included.

➢ *Keyword*

The keyword resume is a variation that adds a listing of skills to the beginning of any standard resume format. Critical occupational skills placed at the beginning add impact to the resume and help capture the reader's attention.

*This resume type is effective for all career fields and skill levels.

The best person to compose your resume is YOU!
You may be told otherwise but coming from someone who does this for others, consider these first before paying someone else to do it for you:

You have all of your experience data

Only you know what you have and haven't done at your former employment. Once you get your information together and choose the wording that you like, you will be able to do it better than anyone else can because you know yourself and your past experience better than anyone! You would have to provide this information to anyone creating your resume for you so why not finish creating it yourself?

You can show off your smarts!

Employers like to see wording on your resume that you would naturally use. Your resume is about you, so format it in your own way and use wording that you would normally use with a few smart words thrown in there that you now use in your everyday vocabulary. I have seen many resumes that are formatted like every other resume, so it is easy for employers to quickly find the information that they need, but at the same time, they put something a little out of the norm to catch the eye. That being said- always use plenty of discretion when doing this so that your resume always appears ultra-professional.

You will need to make revisions often

Consider that you may make numerous changes and additions to your resume as you compile it as well as while you are keeping your information current. It's very important that you have the ability to access your resume and make the changes yourself or it may be very costly to revise it when you are having someone else do it for you and I promise you, there will be many necessary revisions as you keep it current throughout your life! Plus, you certainly don't want to be waiting on someone else's schedule in order to revise your resume when you need to be doing your job search.

It's easy to do!

It is very easy to create your own resume with all of the wonderful new choices in resume software that we have available to us and you can always type it up yourself by using the example chronological format that I provide in my course. This one is the most standard format, there are other formats and you should take the time to decide which is best for you to highlight your experience in the best light possible.

Look at resumes through the employer's eyes for a moment:

If you were looking to fill a position in your department and let's say you receive 55 resumes through your excellent recruiting, you are not going to have time to interview everyone. You would decide to do what most employers do and make a "quick scan" of each resume and place the resume's aside that are not worth interview time. I call this the "No pile."

In this scenario you would only want to interview 5-10 final candidates. This is why it is so important that your resume shows your skill set for the particular job that you are applying for at a quick glance. They don't have time to review anything more than basic requirements and appearance. Catch their eye!

Hints to creating that perfect resume!

Keep it current!

♦ Always keep your resume current so that you feel ready no matter what happens with layoffs, etc., for your own mental security. You also don't want to be scrambling to get your information together in a time crunch.

Objective

When to be more specific

♦ If you have an objective on your resume, state the exact job title if:
  • You are responding to a specific advertisement.
  • You have specific fields of interest.
  • You are applying with companies within the same field.

When to be more general

♦ You are going to want to keep it more generally versed if:
  • You are going to send your resume to a variety of companies.
  • You are unsure about future fields of interest.
  • You don't want to keep making changes to your objective.

Many people choose to leave out the objective in their resumes and that is perfectly acceptable! If you do want to use an objective, a good tip is to develop an objective that is beneficial to both you and the employer.

Volunteer experience
- ♦ Use volunteer experience on the resume just like your employment experience. Volunteer experience is a fabulous way to show off the content of your character and it is counted the same as work experience!

Hobbies
- ♦ Include your hobbies or personal interests as long as they are not controversial and you have extra space. Some studies show that you can be offered up to $3,000.00 more per year by doing so! If you do include them, list them in their own category.

Be honest!
- ♦ Ensure integrity with your resume by being honest but at the same time showing off only your best! Lying or exaggerating your abilities will always come back to haunt you! Employers usually check with the references you list as well as the previous supervisors you list when you are considered a serious candidate so you will want every detail to check out. Make sure that your resume will hold up to scrutiny.

Quick Tip!

If you are unsure of what keywords might be right for your resume, you can scan the classifieds for various employment positions that are similar to the ones that you are interested in. Notice which words are coming up repeatedly and use those that apply to you! Pay attention to keywords interviewers in your field are using as well! Using the keywords for these skills and traits ensure that you are-
"Just exactly what they are looking for!"

Over-qualification?

- ◆ *If you are being made to answer for being overqualified, take a closer look at your resume to make sure that you have targeted it correctly.*
  - • *Have you chosen the correct resume format for the job you are looking for?*
  - • *Do you need to leave something out that does not pertain to the position?*
  - • *Have you targeted your resume to the employment level you are seeking?*

If you target your resume correctly, you will be more effective in convincing them that this job is right for you and you are the right person for the job.

Always use quality paper

- ◆ Don't skimp here, how you look on paper may be the difference between getting the call for an interview or not.

- ◆ Use quality resume paper, never exotic or unique paper types, keep it professional.

- ◆ Be careful with colored paper. Only use subtle, professional looking resume paper colors.

Charts

- ◆ Do not include charts or graphs. These are unnecessary in the resume.

Keep the positive- lose the negative!

- ◆ Your resume should never state anything negative, when in doubt- leave it out!

Unmentionables!

♦ Do not mention age, race, religion, sex, national origin, marital status, health or physical description like height, weight, etc. Employers cannot even legally ask this information during an interview so there is no need to offer it!

♦ Do not mention weaknesses or things done wrong.

♦ Do not make demands on your resume.

♦ Do not make references to availability.

♦ Do not place reasons for leaving employment on the resume.

♦ Never include a written testimonial.

♦ Avoid verifiable exaggerations as they can quickly cost you your job.

♦ Do not use humor or clichés in resumes.

Use the appropriate resume format!

♦ Show off your good points such as years at the same job by making sure that the resume format you choose is the right type for you. Chronological type is the normal type that most job seekers use. You may read further about the different resume types and how they are used in this chapter.

High School

♦ Do not list your high school on your resume unless you are very young and need more filler. If you are an adult who has not been to college, for me it just screams that you haven't been to college if you list your high school on your resume.

Photographs

♦ Don't place pictures on your resume unless you are applying for a modeling position and even in that case, I would suggest that you give them a well prepared portfolio of yourself instead. Pictures on resumes are very outdated and unprofessional. If you know you look great, excellent- see them in person!

Caps

♦ Never use all caps. It looks unprofessional and presents you as lazy and unintelligent. It is very hard to read a resume if it is created entirely in all capital letters as well.

♦ This is also considered "yelling" or "screaming" the capped sentences when typing in all caps in most cyber forums so it is obviously not very professional!

♦ You should use caps to highlight information only, such as job and title, etc.

Show that you are focused

♦ Let your resume show you as consistent-- climbing the ladder in the same field is preferable, if you are changing fields entirely; make sure you have an excellent reason for it!

Salary

♦ Never mention salary on your resume. The interview is the only appropriate place to mention salary expectations. (You will be asked to list it on the application but before doing so, make sure that you have read the part in this course about applications and salary expectations!)

♦ Never mention any previous wages on the resume. This is listed on the application.

Proof, proof, proof!

♦ Spend lots of time proofreading and perfecting your resume! Spell check often and watch for grammatical errors but do not solely rely on spell check programs as sometimes a word may be spelled incorrectly for the meaning you were going for, but the spell check feature will not see this as a wrong word because the incorrectly spelled word is a word as well on its own. Words can also sound the same but are not spelled the same. Always have someone proof read your resume that is good with their spelling and grammar.

Time gaps?

♦ If you need to de-emphasize glaring gaps in your work history, you might want to consider using a functional type of resume format, which focuses on your skills and accomplishments rather than a chronological format, which emphasizes the progression of your experience. Consider all resume types before creating your own to ensure that you are portrayed in the best possible light!

♦ Time gaps need to be accounted for. They can be disguised on the resume but always be prepared to account for it with a positive statement during an interview!

Wording!

♦ Use excellent words on your resume that are unique to your work personality! You seem much more interesting!

♦ Use spectacular yet true sentences!

♦ Start with your strongest statements!

♦ Clearly communicate your purpose and value to the employer in words they can relate with.

♦ Place fabulous keywords throughout your resume. Do not continually use the same keywords- vary your wording. You can choose from many words listed in this course.

♦ Never come across as arrogant on your resume, confident wording is the key.

♦ Never use slang wording. This can make you seem childish and very unprofessional. It also clearly takes your perceived intelligence down a few notches!

♦ Do not change the tense of verbs you use in the resume- keep it consistent.

♦ Write your own resume. Be personal, yet professional. Create a resume that is personalized to reflect you.

Quick Tip!

Always be positive about yourself on your resume! Remove any negative comments or feelings conveyed in your resume, especially when it comes to previous employment experiences. Emphasize a positive, can-do attitude. They want to see your confidence on paper!

- Do not get too specific, no one is really that interested. Use the fewest possible words. Remember, we are trying to keep it to one page only. You may use the front and back of one page but I don't recommend two or more pages.

- Use action verbs! Words like created, managed, directed, launched, etc. Portray yourself as active, accomplished, intelligent and capable of making a contribution. For example: "Mastered two word processing programs: WordPerfect and Microsoft Word" or "Successfully increased regional sales by 1.2 million" have impact. Notice how using action words have strengthened these statements.

- Using industry jargon and acronyms reflect your familiarity with the employer's business, but use them sparingly so that your resume is still very easy to read.

- Why does the employer need you? Focus on highlighting accomplishments that will arouse the interest of employers who read resumes asking themselves: "What can this candidate do for me?" Remember that the goal is to get an interview.

- "Civilianize" your military language, (e.g., NCOIC to Supervisor.) Always convert military terms into civilian terms that the employer can understand.

- Do not use abbreviations in your sentences. You should use them only for directions such as S for south or the middle initial of your name.

- Avoid personal pronouns. Never use personal pronouns such as "I" or "me" in your resume. Instead of using complete sentences, consider using short, action-oriented phrases such as: "Coordinated and published a weekly newsletter concerning local community events," rather than using personal pronouns.

- Emphasize your skills. Use a skill-based resume format that is organized around the main talents you have to offer. Prioritize your skills to what the interviewer would view as relevant to the position.

♦ Include specific keywords and phrases that describe your skill and experience, such as Income Statement, Balance Sheet, Sales Account Management, Visual Basic, Word Processing, MS Excel, MS Word, Adobe Illustrator, Graphic Design, Advertising, Personnel Management, etc.

♦ List only your recent employment information. The general rule of thumb is to show your work experience only for the last 10 to 15 years. The application usually asks for you to list the last five jobs you have had.

♦ Employers love to see numbers that make sense! Numbers are a powerful tool. Instead of saying "Responsible for increasing sales in my territory," use "Increased sales in my territory by 150% in 6 months" or "Managed 14 accounts for annual revenues of over $1m." Focus on measurable accomplishments from your prior experience that are relevant to the employer.

♦ Shorten sentences by taking out articles like "a," "an," "the" etc. For example, if your original sentence is "Responsibilities include the installation and maintenance of networking software products." Take out the word "the" and the sentence is just as powerful. "Responsibilities include installation and maintenance of networking software products," or "Supervision of a night secretarial staff" can be changed to "Supervision of night secretarial staff," etc.

♦ Don't utilize extreme vocabulary. Don't try to impress employers with the depth of your vocabulary. Use words everyone can understand. There are some great example words to choose from in this chapter to help you make the best impression!

♦ Do not under-emphasize your strengths and experience. We all have skills that we can use for future employment. (Including transferable skills!) Portray yourself in the best possible light. There are skills that may come naturally to you that others may never grasp. Make sure that the personal skills and traits about yourself that you choose to list might be considered valuable to the new employer.

References

♦ Don't include your references on your resume. These should be shown to the employer separately from your resume. Make sure to contact each reference that you use to ask their permission to use them as a reference before doing so!

♦ I don't even recommend placing "References available upon request" on the resume. This is very outdated and employers expect references anyway. You do not need to waste space on your resume for that.

Document titles

♦ Do not include titles on documents for the document itself such as: resume, fact sheet, curriculum, cover letter, etc. There is no reason to label documents as most are self-explanatory.

Formatting

♦ Formatting is very important! I can spend hours on formatting alone as formatting can make any document easier to read, and make it appear much more interesting. It is always worth your extra efforts for that final presentation!

Visual Impact!

Keep your resume to only one page

♦ Use the front and back if you need, but summarize your information. While electronic resumes may exceed the traditional one to two page limit of paper resumes, in most cases, it should not exceed three pages when sent in digital format.

♦ Varying your sentence structure using bullets to support original sentences makes it easier and more interesting to read.

♦ Use an easy-to-read format. The easier it is to read, the more likely the employer is to actually read it!

♦ Clean it up! Your resume should appear neat, well organized and professional.

- Make a good first impression. On average, employers spend less than 30 seconds scanning each resume. Most employers are more concerned about career achievements than education. Place the most interesting and compelling facts about yourself at the beginning, such as "List of accomplishments" in order of relevance.

- Send your resume flat in a large white envelope whenever mailing it to an employer.

- Do not fold, staple or otherwise bind your resume.

- Clearly indicate your contact information at a glance!

- Using one inch margins enhances the readability of your resume.

Font

- Choose a font type that is easy to read. (Times New Roman is a good one) Never use script or fancy font types. You always want your resume professional looking and easy to read.

- The best font size for any document to be easily read by most people is a size 12. Any font size between a 10 and 14 is appropriate for a resume.

Jist cards

- Use a jist card to make your resume stand out from other resumes.

- Making your jist card the same color as your resume is preferred for a more uniform, polished look.

- Think of the jist card as a miniature resume and business card combined. You can pass it out by itself when networking if you choose.

Cover Letters

- Always include a cover letter when sending your resume to a potential employer by mail, e-mail, fax, etc.

- Keep your cover letters brief!

Printing

♦ Use a good quality laser printer to print out your final copy. If you use a dot matrix printer, the wording could bleed or blur when handled or if it accidentally gets wet. It's worth a few extra pennies to have a great final copy!

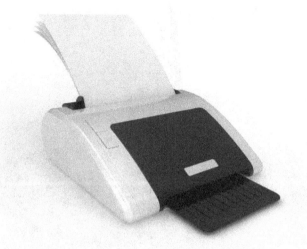

Quick Tip!

Review your resume many times before sending it out! Have two more people besides yourself take a look at it and give you their feedback. In addition to reviewing your experience, employers also use the resume to get a sense of whether you are organized and logical. They also check to see if you are making typos and spelling errors which are considered a huge red flag before they ever consider calling you in for an interview.

Use a good word processing software program to create your resume

♦ A good word processor will allow you to view and correct almost all spelling and grammar errors you may make.

♦ You can easily make changes to the resume whenever you need to with your software.

♦ Most jobs require that you have worked with word processing software. They are very easy to use. Get familiar with them by using one to create your resume, cover letters, etc. You can also purchase tutorial CD's to help you quickly learn the software. Once you have learned it, the added benefit is that you may list it as one of your skills! Choose a software program that most employers are familiar with and is easy to use such as MS Word, etc.

♦ With a good software program, you can easily convert your paper resume format into a plain text resume format for sending electronically.

Sending your resume electronically

Quick Tip!

When sending your resume electronically to online databases etc. I recommend that you keep your home address private and off of your resume entirely. No one needs to know that information. List your two forms of contact information as a home or cell phone number and e-mail address only. You may also want to keep your current employers phone number confidential so that they do not find out that you are looking for another job by getting a call from a prospective employer!

PLAIN TEXT RESUMES

Once you have mastered the paper resume, you should absolutely create a second, plain text resume. You will be asked to e-mail your resume by many employers and once you're done creating it, you can also post your resume in employment databases online. On the internet there are numerous opportunities to present your resume to potential employers. You can even set up a professional website using your resume information if you choose.

Many times you will need to send your resume electronically by request of the employer. The problem with that however, is that the resume may look quite different upon receipt from the format in which you sent it. You want it to look as nice as possible!

How to create your plain text resume

You can create a new resume in whatever software program you are using, (or use a copy of your existing resume) and then go to the "Save As" option in your software program (under the file menu) and save the new resume as text/ASCII and rename the new document at the same time.

(If you use the "Save As" option rather than the "Save" option, you now still have your first resume but you also have your new resume as well.)

At this point, the new resume document will look really badly formatted but this way you can reformat it to look a lot nicer and save it again when you are done reformatting in plain text. Send the new version you have created to employers electronically instead.

Quick Tip!

FORMATTING PLAIN TEXT RESUMES
Formatting is very important for the overall effect! Most formatting such as bold, italics, underlining, shading, lines and graphics can be lost when sending an electronic resume so you are limited as far as formatting. Here are some tips of what you can use to format the plain text resume:

- ◆ *Highlight key points*
- ◆ *Use capital letters to highlight only section titles and work titles.*
- ◆ *Use quotation marks for emphasis.*
- ◆ *You can use the asterisk as a great bullet mark. Always place a space between the asterisk and the text.*
- ◆ *Remember that e-mail only allows for 70 characters per line so reformat the text per line as well.*

When formatting your resume, make sure to be balanced and neat. The effective resume is balanced, neat, visually appealing and flows consistently. You want it to be easily read. Make sure to clearly separate sections and emphasize section titles. Leave sufficient blank space between sections for easy reading as well.

Most computer programs can read plain text resumes so you should be able to send it to almost anyone electronically once you are finished creating it! In this technological world, it is a must that you have both the paper and electronic resume.

Website resumes

Some software programs will allow you to also save your original resume as an HTML (Hypertext Markup Language) document which will allow for it to be able to translate the data into words, format, color as well as graphics. HTML is the markup language used for creating documents on the World Wide Web. You can create your own professional website resume, it is an extensive topic but there are many helps online and in book stores on how to create websites or you can pay a professional to create one for you. Make sure that you keep it separate from your "personal" website! The tips for writing resumes also apply if you choose to create a website resume.

Faxing your resume

Before faxing your resume to a prospective employer, send a test fax to yourself so that you can see how your faxed version is received. It may surprise you as to how many pages long it is! Keep your faxed version as short as possible just as you would your paper resume.

Your resume should ONLY make you shine! Everything else shows up on the application. It's worth it to pay a professional to prepare your resume who really knows the difference!

Critiquing your Resume

When you are done composing your resume, critique your work. Ask yourself these questions to be sure you have done your best:

- ♦ Has it been proofed by at least one other person than yourself?
- ♦ Is the general appearance good?
- ♦ Is it easy to read at a glance?
- ♦ Do you have the correct resume format?
- ♦ How many skills are displayed?
- ♦ Can you cut out sentences in your resume?
- ♦ Can you cut out paragraphs in your resume?
- ♦ Where have you repeated yourself?
- ♦ Does the content focus towards the occupation of your choice?
- ♦ Are there any grammar or spelling errors?
- ♦ Is it too long or too short?
- ♦ Is it an honest representation of who you are at your best?

Proofreading your final draft
Go back to it! Leave it for a day and then re-read it fresh.
Always have someone else proofread it when you are done so that you have a second pair of eyes looking over your finished product.

Always keep it current!
If you keep the information on your data organizer and resume current, you will feel a lot more confident whenever you need to conduct another job search!

Sculpting your Resume!

HEADINGS you can choose from to create your perfect resume and jist card!

Accomplishments
Accomplishments & Achievements
Accreditations & Licenses
Achievements
Achievements and Results
Activities
Additional
Additional Expertise
Additional Information
Additional Professional Training
Additional Training
Affiliations
Appointments
Areas of Effectiveness
Areas of Expertise
Areas of Impact
Awards
Background
Background Summary
Business Experience
Capabilities
Career Highlights
Career History
Career Objective
Career Profile
Certificates
Certifications
Civil Service Grades
Communications Knowledge
Community Activities
Computer Languages

Computer Skills
Computer Systems
Continuing Education
Education
Education & Training
Education & Vocational Skills
Educational Background
Educational History
Employment
Employment Experience
Employment Goal
Employment Objective
Employment Progression
Equipment
Examinations
Executive Summary
Exhibitions & Awards
Experience
Experience Highlights
Extra-Curricular Activities
Field of Experience
Field of Interest
Fields of Interest
Fieldworks
Government Experience
Highlights
Highlights of Qualifications
Hobbies
Honors
Honors & Awards
Interests

Headings Continued...

Interests & Hobbies
Involvements
Job Objective
Job Target
Key Qualifications
Knowledge/Skills
Languages
Licenses
Licenses and Certifications
Licensure/Certifications
Licensures
Military Experience
Military Training Summaries
Objective
Offering
Other Achievements
Other Facts
Outside Interests
Patents
Patents & Publications
Personal
Personal Data
Personal Information
Position Desired
Presentations/Publications
Previous Experience and
Accomplishments
Principle Skills
Professional Affiliations
Professional Associates
Professional Attributes
Professional Background
Professional Experience
Professional Experience and
Accomplishments

Professional Goals
Professional Interest
Professional Memberships
Professional Objective
Professional Organizations
Professional Profile
Proven Capabilities
Proven Experiences
Proven Value
Proven Worth
Publications
Publications & Patents
Qualifications
Qualifications Summary
Registration
Related Accomplishments
Related Capabilities
Related Experiences
Related Skills
Representative List of Clients
Security Clearance
Selected Achievements
Selected Achievements & Results
Significant Accomplishments
Skill Set
Skill Summary
Skills
Skills/Experience
Societies
Software
Special Activities
Special Skills
Special Strengths
Special Training
Strengths

Headings Continued...

Success Patterns	*Target Job*
Successes	*Technical Skills*
Successful Experiences	*Training*
Summary	*Vocational Target*
Summary of Background	*Volunteer/Community Service*
Summary of Experience	*Volunteer Experience*
Summary of Knowledge & Experience	*Volunteer Work*
Summary of Qualifications	*Work Experience*
Summary of Skills	*Work History*
Summary of Supportive Qualifications	*Work & Volunteer Experience*
Summer Jobs	*Work Objective*
Supporting Skills	*Workshops and Seminars*

Fabulous Wording!

Use these gems liberally when sculpting your resume and in person during interviews.
Use any of these words for designing your jist card as well!

Accept responsibility	Compare	Dedicated
Accept supervision	Compare data	Delegate
Accomplished	Competent	Delivered
Accurate	Competitive	Demonstrate
Achieved	Compile	Dependable
Achiever	Compile statistics	Design
Administered	Complete	Detail
Administrator	Compose	Detail oriented
Advise	Comprehend	Detected
Agility	Comprehensive	Determine
Ambitious	Compute	Develop
Analyze	Conceive	Develop rapport
Appraise	Conceptualize	Develop support
Approved	Conducted	Develop trust
Arranged	Conflict management	Developer
Ask questions	Conflict resolution	Diplomacy
Assertive	Consistent	Diplomatic
Assess situations	Construct	Direct
Assisted	Consult	Directed
Assume responsibility	Consulting	Discovered
Balancing	Control	Dispense
Bilingual	Converse	Disproved
Broad	Cooperative	Distributed
Budget	Coordinate	Diversity
Budgeting	Coordinator	Divert
Build	Copy	Do precision work
Calculate	Counsel	Drawing
Capable	Count	Drive
Caring	Created	Dynamic
Chart information	Creative	Economize
Check for accuracy	Debate	Edited
Classify	Decision making	Effective
Comforting	Decisive	Efficient
Communicate	Decreased	Eliminated

Fabulous Wording Continued...

Quick Tip!

Pay particular attention to the words that are considered "action verbs" which can make you sound even more capable and interesting!

Empathy
Encourage
Endurance
Energy
Enlarged
Entertain
Enthusiastic
Establish priorities
Established
Estimate
Evaluate
Evaluated
Examine
Excelled
Exchange
Exhibit
Expand
Expedite
Explain
Explore
Extensive
Fast learner
File
Financial analysis
Financial management
Finishing
Fiscal analysis
Flexible
Focus
Follow instructions
Follow through

Formulated
Founded
Friendly
Gather
Generalist
Generated
Get things done
Group facilitating
Guided
Handle
Headed
Help
Highly motivated
Hire/fire
Honesty
Identified
Implemented
Improved
Increase productivity
Increase profits
Influence
Inform
Ingenious
Initiated
Innovate
Inquiry
Inspected
Inspire
Installed
Instituted
Instructed

Integrity
Intelligent
Intensive
Interpreted
Interview
Introduced
Invented
Inventive
Inventory
Investigate
Judgment
Juggling
Justified
Keep books
Keyboard
Kind
Launched
Lead
Leader
Learn
Learn quickly
Lectured
Led
Listening
Locate
Log information
Made
Maintained
Make decisions
Make policy
Manage crisis

Fabulous Wording Continued...

Manage money	*Presented*	*Results oriented*
Managed	*Prided*	*Reviewed*
Manager	*Problem solver*	*Revised*
Manipulate	*Processed*	*Risk taker*
Mature	*Produced*	*Sales*
Measure	*Proficiency*	*Schedule*
Mediate	*Program*	*Select*
Meet deadlines	*Programmed*	*Self-motivated*
Mentor	*Project*	*Sell*
Modify	*Project planning*	*Sense of direction*
Monitored	*Promote*	*Sense of humor*
Motivate people	*Proposed*	*Sensitive*
Motivated	*Provided*	*Sequence*
Motivating	*Public speaking*	*Served*
Motivator	*Punctual*	*Set up*
Negotiate	*Purchase*	*Sew*
Nurture	*Purpose*	*Signal*
Observe	*Raise money*	*Sincere*
Obtained	*Recommended*	*Skilled*
Operated	*Record*	*Sociable*
Ordered	*Recruit*	*Sold*
Organized	*Rectify*	*Solid*
Outgoing	*Reduced*	*Solve problems*
Patient	*Referred*	*Solved*
Perform music	*Refinishing*	*Sort*
Persistent	*Reliable*	*Sparked*
Persuaded	*Reorganized*	*Speak*
Physically strong	*Repair*	*Specialist*
Plan	*Replaced*	*Specific*
Planning	*Reported*	*Strategic*
Plant	*Represented*	*Streamlined*
Pleasant	*Research*	*Strengthened*
Practice	*Respect*	*Studied*
Precise	*Responsible*	*Successful*
Precision	*Responsive*	*Summarize*
Prepared	*Restore*	*Supervise*

Fabulous Wording Continued...

Supplier	*Tend*	*Understood*
Supply	*Thorough*	*Updated*
Survey	*Tolerance*	*Upgraded*
Sympathy	*Tolerant*	*Urgency*
Synthesize	*Tough*	*Utilized*
Systematic	*Trained*	*Verified*
Tabulate	*Trainer*	*Willing to learn*
Tactful	*Translated*	*Willing worker*
Take instruction	*Trimmed*	*Won*
Taking inventory	*Troubleshooter*	*Work as a team member*
Talented	*Trusting*	*Work well under pressure*
Taught	*Trustworthy*	*Write*
Teach	*Understanding*	*Wrote*

128

CHRONOLOGICAL RESUME EXAMPLE WORKSHEET

_____   _____
Name   **Home Phone**

_____   _____
Address   **Message/Work Phone**

Career Objective

_____

_____

Experience

_____ -- _____   _____
Dated From   To   **Name of the position that you held at the company**

_____
Company name and location (City, State)

_____
Explanation of position held/duties performed

_____
Responsibilities within the company

_____
My accomplishments

Education

_____ -- _____   _____
From   To   **Degree obtained**

_____
Name of school you attended and location (City, State)

_____
Personal achievements, etc.

"FUNCTIONAL" TYPE RESUME EXAMPLE WORKSHEET

_____
(Name)
_____
(Street Address)
_____
(City, State and Zip Code)
_____
(Phone Number)

Objective
_____
_____

Summary
_____
_____

Sales Experience_____
(Sales statement) _____

Management Experience
_____
(Management statement) _____

Production _____
(Production statement) _____

WORK EXPERIENCE

_____--_____   _____
Dates (to and from)   (Company name and address)
                          _____
                                    (Your title)

_____--_____   _____
Dates (to and from)   (Company name and address)
                          _____
                                    (Your title)

_____--_____   _____
Dates (to and from)   (Company name and address)
_____ _____   _____
                                    (Your title)

EDUCATION

_____
(Degree, graduate date and title of school)

130

"COMBINATION" TYPE RESUME EXAMPLE WORKSHEET

_____
(Name)
_____
(Street Address)
_____
(City, State and Zip Code)
_____
(Phone Number)

OBJECTIVE:

_____
_____

SUMMARY: _____
_____

SALES EXPERIENCE: _____
(Sales statement) _____

MANAGEMENT: _____
(Management statement) _____

MARKETING: _____
(Marketing statement) _____

FINANCIAL: _____
(Financial work statement) _____

EXPERIENCE

_____ -- _____   _____
Dates (to and from)   (Company name and address)
                       _____
                                         (Your title)
_____
_____
_____
_____
                       (Statement of work responsibilities)

Additional Responsibilities:

♦ _____
♦ _____
♦ _____

131

_____ -- _____   _____
Dates (to and from)   (Company name and address)

                         _____
                                         (Your title)

_____
_____
_____
_____
_____
                         (Statement of work responsibilities)

Additional Responsibilities:
(Bullets if preferred)
- _____
- _____
- _____

_____ -- _____   _____
Dates (to and from)   (Company name and address)

                         _____
                                         (Your title)

_____
_____
_____
_____
                         (Statement of work responsibilities)

Additional Responsibilities:
(Bullets if preferred)
- _____
- _____
- _____

Talents:

Effective communicating, team leader, discretion, word processing, personnel management, training, arbitration, spreadsheets, quality control, inventory, cleanliness, details, negotiation, diplomacy.

HIGH SCHOOL RESUME EXAMPLE WORKSHEET

PERSONAL INFORMATION

_____
Name

_____
Address

_____
Phone Number

SCHOOL

_____
High School Name

_____
High School Address

_____
High School Phone Number

LEADERSHIP POSITIONS HELD IN SCHOOL

_____
Class Offices (President, Student judge, Class representative, etc.)

_____
Clubs (Treasurer, Secretary, etc.)

_____
Extracurricular Activities

MEMBERSHIPS, CLUBS, VOLUNTEER WORK and OTHER ACTIVITIES
(In school and outside of school)

_____

_____

HONORS and AWARDS

_____

COLLEGE RESUME EXAMPLE WORKSHEET

PERSONAL INFORMATION

_____
Name

_____
Permanent Address

_____
Phone Number

SCHOOL

_____
College/University

_____
School Address and Phone

_____
Major

ACADEMIC EXPERIENCE
_____
_____

WORK EXPERIENCE
_____
_____

MILITARY SERVICE
_____
_____

VOLUNTEER WORK
_____
_____

MEMBERSHIPS, CLUBS
_____
_____

HOBBIES, SPORTS
_____
_____

AWARDS and HONORS
_____
_____

Jist Cards
Your mini resume!

A jist card is a combination of a resume and a business card in one!

The next few pages are just a few examples of different types of jist cards. You can design yours using any heading you choose in the resume section.

Get creative with your wording! This is YOUR jist card, you can say anything you want!

Quick Tip!

A jist card is like a tiny resume and business card combined. It's a fabulous way to introduce yourself and your skillset to an employer in 30 seconds!
An excellent job search tool!

A jist card usually includes:

Your name
Telephone number
Email address
Skills
Accomplishments
Personal assets/Work related

- ♦ **You can choose from your favorite headings in the list for resume headings to make your jist card work perfect for you!**

- ♦ **Use a thick (cardstock) paper in the same color as your resume for the jist card.**

- ♦ **You should be able to fit about four jist cards per page if formatted correctly**

Andy Smith   (123) 456-7890

Email: mye@mail.com

Web Designer

Two years' experience developing websites for commercial as well as nonprofit organizations. Fluent in HTML, XML, XHTML, WML, e-Commerce, Unix, and Open Source.

Excellent troubleshooting skills
Willing to work any hours

Efficient   Self-motivated   Detail Oriented   Dedicated

Trent Talent   (123) 456-7890

Field of Interest: Hotel/Hospitality

Skills: Worked as a Night Auditor for three years and successfully worked with a windows based as well as a DOS based system. Capable of quickly mastering any software program placed before me.

Accomplishments: Successfully trained many other associates regarding each software program. Taking great care to ensure the safety and satisfaction of all guests, I continually demonstrated the ability to intuitively anticipate the guests' needs while ensuring the highest level of standards regarding customer service and cleanliness.

Motivated about the industry

Resourcefulness Integrity Innovation Precision Teamwork Vision

---

Pakine Leea   (123) 456-7890

Field of Interest: Employment Recruiter

Skills: MS Works, MS Word, Excel, Power Point, Access, 40 wpm. Disciplined, Motivated, Precision, Decisive, Exceptional eye for talent.

Accomplishments: Written two books regarding the work of recruiting for companies and how to successfully choose the best applicants for your companies' needs. Found numerous employees for companies in need of the best people for their respective business types.

Finding the right person for the job is priceless!

INTEGRITY VISION PROFESSIONALISM EXTRORDINARY INTUITION

Jack Johnson   (123) 456-7890
                                    Email: mye@mail.com

Field of Interest: Hotel/Hospitality

Areas of Expertise: Over 21 years in the hospitality industry effectively demonstrating the ability to fulfill guests needs even in the most extreme of circumstances. Consistent and precise, my work ethic is measured by the satisfaction of each individual guest.

Exceptional Talents: Polishing and mastering my management capabilities, I am familiar and thorough with all aspects of keeping a hotel successfully operating at full capacity, including property maintenance, training associates and resolving guest issues of all kinds. With exceptional staff guidance and understanding, department productivity is increased to maximum levels! Helping associates to excel, each in their individual capacities. Motivating employees and promoting a teamwork environment where each individual feels valued and recognized for their efforts is naturally obtained through my encouraging style of leadership.

Excel under pressure

CAPABLE   RELIABLE   DETAIL ORIENTED   DECISIVE   PRECISE

Debbie Jones   **(123) 456-7890**

Caregiver/Recreational Therapist

Patient and understanding, I have dedicated 27 years of my life to caring for and serving the needs of others. With tact and decorum, I can ensure the highest of respectability in regards to caring for the needs of your loved ones. I have a solid background of dependable and dedicated service.

Excellent References

Tactful   Dependable   Respectful   Understanding   Kindness

Rick Diamond   Phone: (123) 456-7890
                             Email: mye@mail.com

Position Desired: General Office/Clerical

More than four years of work experience plus one year of training in office practices. Trained in word processing, Type 50 wpm, have good interpersonal skills, and enjoy working with the general public.

Can meet deadlines and handle pressure well

Motivated   Clear Thinking   Fast Learner

How to use jist cards:

♦ You should have them with you whenever contacting the employer.

♦ You can take them to interviews with you to introduce your resume quickly by passing them out along with your resume. (Paper clipping it to the top of your resume works great!)

♦ You can take them with you when filling out applications and leave them for the potential employer together with your resume and/or application.

♦ You can give them out liberally at job fairs

♦ Whenever giving thank you notes or follow up correspondence with the employer, place the jist card together with the thank you note in the envelope. This is used as a reminder of your worth to them!

♦ You can send a digital photo copy of your jist card together with your resume or paste it into the body of any type of e-mail correspondence with the potential employer.

Design your jist card with your favorite Transferable skills & Self-Management skills that describe the person that is uniquely *YOU!*

JIST CARD EXAMPLE WORKSHEET

_____   _____
Your name   Home Phone

_____   _____
Your chosen target heading   Employment objective

_____   _____
Your chosen valuable heading   Statement regarding your experience

                                          _____
                                          Statement regarding your education

                                          _____
                                          Statement regarding your job-related skills

_____
Statement regarding your problem solving skills

_____
Statement regarding your self-management skills

Many job seekers use a jist card to enhance their resume. This is a basic example of a jist card. You can create your own jist card in any format that you choose that will showcase your skills, just remember to keep it small! This card should always be 3x5" or smaller. (2 ½x4" -just slightly bigger than business card size is perfect!) It should complement your resume, not swallow it up!

Quick Tip!

The jist card is to be paper clipped to the top of your resume and presented to the employer together with your resume. It is utilized to give the employer more information about you professionally as well as a few personal items can be listed here if you so choose. (Such as your hobbies) Presenting your resume with an attached jist card helps ensure that your resume stands out from the rest! Place your five key words that best describe your best self professionally at the bottom of the card in bold for extra emphasis!

Skill Statements

These are statements that show proof of your skills by using examples which can be very powerful! They are your personal positive skills and are invaluable. They can be skills that you have learned from work experience, volunteer experience, your life experience or any transferable skills.

Workshop!

1. *Choose five of your favorite skill words to describe you best. You may use the lists of words provided that are proven to be effective.*

Now we will expand each individual skill you have chosen and show an example for each skill. Create a statement about each of your skills linking these examples of favorite skills to what the employer is looking for.

2. Form statements utilizing each key skill word that describes you effectively.

Here are some examples of skills and statements:

Skill: *"I can meet deadlines."*

Statement: *"While in school, I rarely missed a due date on an assignment." "If I was able to meet deadlines in school, I will also be able to meet your work deadlines."*

Skill: *"I am good with budgeting expenses"*

Skill Statement: *"I have successfully budgeted the expenses of an entire household of five for the last nine years. I will be able to apply these skills when reviewing and planning the budget of this department."*

Skill: *"I am a good communicator"*

Statement: *"My work as a telemarketer required me to communicate with a diverse array of people, some of whom represented difficult challenges. I refined my communication skills to the point where I was nearly always able to smooth ruffled feathers, solve problems, and provide satisfaction to customers. These are exactly the skills that are vital to effective hotel management, and I am eager to apply my talents at your hotel."*

Skill: *"I am a patient problem solver"*

Statement: *"As a sales associate in a retail store, I successfully handled the daily needs of individual customers. To succeed, I had to be a patient and diplomatic problem-solver. Because the same kinds of patience and creative problem-solving are required of teachers, I am confident I will be an effective second-grade teacher at your school."*

Skill: *"I am intuitive"*

Statement: *"I am very intuitive with others. I have found this skill very valuable when dealing with different character types of the general public. I have been able to avoid problems by anticipating the needs of others." "I am willing to put this skill to good use when I am dealing with customers at this position."*

Skill: *"I am dependable"*

Statement: *"I am very dependable. I have not missed a day of work for the past year. I actually enjoy working and I see the value of keeping busy." "I am someone that you will be able to depend on to be here every day."*

Now turn your favorite skills into sentences by stating the skill, then showing an example of how you use the skill and next, linking the skill to the current job you are applying for.

Quick Tip!

Speak in the present tense to show that your skills are current and applicable in today's market!

SKILL #1: _____

STATEMENT:

_____

_____

SKILL #2: _____

STATEMENT:

_____

_____

SKILL #3: _____

STATEMENT:

_____

_____

SKILL #4: _____

STATEMENT:

_____

_____

Quick Tip!

Back up every skill you mention by having a statement that shows how you have used it. This is especially impressive if you are stating a general skill that most applicants will use like "I am dependable" etc. You will be more believed and remembered for having that skill above other applicants if you back it up!

Even if you haven't had a lot of employment experience, you always have transferable skills! Here are some examples:

➢ *Someone coming straight out of school probably knows how to attain goals, how to multitask, meet deadlines, etc.*

➢ *Someone who has spent time as a server has marketing skills because when a customer asks about the food or when telling them about the special, you need to sell it to them!*

➢ *Someone coming straight from homemaking work such as mothers coming back to the work force have all kinds of transferable skills, including; budgeting, multitasking, time management, leadership, organizational skills, and communication talents just to name a few!*

➢ *A young person who plays on the computer a lot is probably more advanced than they realize with their computer skills that may be applied at various positions. This type of person should take an inventory of their computer skills, software that they are familiar with, etc.*

➢ *Even a person who has managed something as simple as a lemonade stand had to learn many transferable skills in order to perform the job. The basic duties might have included production, marketing, distribution and financial management. There are many skills needed to accomplish these functions, including: mixing, measuring, planning, sales, customer service, writing, cash handling, record keeping, maintenance, dependability, accuracy and motivation. This list of skills could go on and on.*

We each have more skills than we normally acknowledge! Every skill you have is marketable!

Your Successes and Achievements!

<u>*My personal positive statements:*</u>

These are the statements that you made about yourself in the first chapter. You will choose the ones that you placed an asterisk by, indicating that they are rare and place them into your data organizer so that you can review it before each interview. This reminds you of just how great you really are and we need all the confidence we can at that crucial time.

My skills that I enjoy about myself that are considered rare:

_____
_____
_____

My personal interests and hobbies:

_____
_____
_____

My personal and work related successes and achievements:

_____
_____
_____

My work experience statements that I would like to remember for interviews:

_____

_____

_____

30 second statement about myself:

_____

_____

_____

My personal uplifting statements to myself to read prior to interviews:

_____

_____

_____

Write down the answers you would give to each of these questions that are routinely asked during interviews:

What is your worst quality?
(This question is asked often and in many different ways so always know what you will say in response to this one!)

_____

_____

_____

What is your best quality?

_____

_____

_____

Describe a time when you were faced with a difficult customer and how you responded to the challenge:

_____

_____

_____

IMPORTANT NOTES!

_____
_____
_____
_____
_____
_____
_____
_____
_____
_____
_____
_____
_____
_____
_____
_____
_____

*Take the information from these last few pages and place them at the end of your data organizer so that you can reference them before interviews!

Self-Management Skills Checklist

These are examples of skills that you use day to day to get along with others and to survive. There are many other self-management skills that you might be able to come up with to describe yourself to an employer. Self-management skills are the skills that make you absolutely unique. Employers look for these skills to determine how a candidate will fit into the existing organization.

Check any three that you feel definitely describe you as an individual. Place your favorite self-management skills in your data organizer. These skills tell the employer if you will get along well with workers and management already on the job so use them well!

Academic	*Creative*	*Logical*	*Reflective*
Accurate	*Democratic*	*Loyal*	*Reliable*
Active	*Dependable*	*Mature*	*Resourceful*
Adaptable	*Dignified*	*Meticulous*	*Responsible*
Alert	*Easygoing*	*Open-minded*	*Sensible*
Ambitious	*Efficient*	*Optimistic*	*Sensitive*
Artistic	*Energetic*	*Organized*	*Serious*
Assertive	*Enterprising*	*Outgoing*	*Sociable*
Businesslike	*Enthusiastic*	*Patient*	*Spontaneous*
Calm	*Fair-minded*	*Peaceable*	*Stable*
Careful	*Flexible*	*Persevering*	*Steady*
Cautious	*Friendly*	*Pleasant*	*Sympathetic*
Charming	*Generous*	*Poised*	*Tactful*
Cheerful	*Good-natured*	*Polite*	*Teachable*
Clear-thinking	*Helpful*	*Practical*	*Thorough*
Clever	*Honest*	*Precise*	*Thoughtful*
Competent	*Humorous*	*Productive*	*Tolerant*
Confident	*Imaginative*	*Progressive*	*Trustworthy*
Conscientious	*Independent*	*Punctual*	*Understanding*
Conservative	*Industrious*	*Quick*	*Verbal*
Considerate	*Intelligent*	*Rational*	*Versatile*
Cooperative	*Kind*	*Realistic*	*Wise*
Courageous	*Likable*	*Reasonable*	*Witty*

Quick Tip!

Most employers would rather hire someone who is less qualified for the position, but who will fit into the existing organization through their self-management skills, other than hire someone who may potentially cause problems with the existing staff. The reason is, **YOU CAN TRAIN A PERSON TO DO THE JOB, BUT YOU CANNOT CHANGE A PERSON'S PERSONALITY OR LACK OF PEOPLE SKILLS!!**

Transferable Skills

Place a check by all the skills that you feel you have. Then choose the five that you think represents you the most. You could have learned the skills during your education, through a training program, volunteer activities, military experience, paid employment or anywhere else in your general life experience. Many skills can transfer from one experience to another.

Carefully evaluate how your skills transfer into other opportunities.

Adapt to situations	*Create*	*Follow through*
Advertising	*Creative*	*Get along with others*
Analyze data	*Decisive*	*Group facilitating*
Anticipate problems	*Delegate*	*Handle complaints*
Appraise service	*Deliver*	*Handle equipment*
Arrange functions	*Demonstrate*	*Handle money*
Articulate	*Dependable*	*Help people*
Assemble products	*Design*	*Illustrate*
Audit records	*Detail*	*Imaginative*
Balancing	*Detail oriented*	*Imagine solutions*
Bargain/barter	*Detect*	*Implement*
Brainstorming	*Develop*	*Improve*
Budget money	*Diplomacy*	*Improvise*
Build	*Direct others*	*Inspect products*
Buy products/services	*Distribute*	*Inspire*
Calculate numbers	*Do precision work*	*Instruct*
Check for accuracy	*Do public relations work*	*Interpret data*
Collect money	*Draft*	*Interview people*
Communicate	*Drawing*	*Inventive*
Compiling	*Drive*	*Learn quickly*
Complete assignments	*Edit*	*Lift (heavy)*
Compute data	*Efficiency*	*Listen*
Conduct	*Encourage*	*Logical*
Conflict management	*Endure long hours*	*Make policy*
Control costs	*Enforce*	*Manage a business*
Control situations	*Establish*	*Manage people*
Coordinate activities	*Evaluate*	*Mature*
Cope w/deadlines	*Examine*	*Mediate problems*
Correspond w/others	*Financial management*	*Meet the public*
Cost analysis	*Fix/repair*	*Memorize information*
Cost conscious	*Follow directions*	*Mentor others*

Transferable Skills Continued...

Monitor progress
Motivate others
Multitasking
Negotiate agreements
Nurse
Operate equipment
Order goods/supplies
Organize data
Organize people
Organize tasks
Outgoing
Own/operate business
Paint
Patient
Perceive needs
Perform
Perform routine work
Persuade others
Plan
Precise
Prepare materials
Problem solving
Process information
Process materials
Promote
Promotional writing
Protect property
Provide maintenance
Public speaking
Publicity
Question others
Quick thinking
Raise money
Read reference books
Recommend

Record data
Recruit people
Reduce costs
Rehabilitate people
Remember information
Remodeling
Repair
Report information
Research
Resolve problems
Restore
Results oriented
Review
Run meetings
Schedule
Self-directed
Self-motivated
Sell
Sense of direction
Sense of humor
Sensitive
Service customers
Service equipment
Set goals/objectives
Set up equipment
Set up systems
Sew
Sign language
Size up situations
Sketch
Socialize
Solve problems
Sort
Speak in public

Speech writing
Strategic planning
Study
Supervise
Support
Take instructions
Test
Think ahead
Think logically
Tolerant
Track
Train/teach
Transcribe
Translate
Travel
Treat/provide care
Troubleshoot
Tutor
Type
Understand
Unite people
Update information
Use hand-eye coordination
Use words correctly
Verify
Visualize
Volunteer
Willing to learn
Work quickly
Write procedures
Write promo material
Write proposals
Write reports
Write technical work

Tips to creating a DVD resume

A DVD resume only enhances your paper resume and does not take the place of your application or your paper resume. You should always have a paper resume ready to give to the employer as well.

Who would want a DVD resume? Someone who is going into fields like graphic design, etc.

♦ You will need a camera and editing and DVD creation software such as windows movie maker or imovie.

♦ Due to the visual element of the DVD resume, the same rules apply for dressing the part for the interview, your body language, etc. Review these sections in the course before creating your DVD resume.

♦ Do not make a DVD resume unless it makes sense to the employer and you can make it appear professional.

♦ Make a script of what you will say so that you are prepared to be brief but do not attempt to read the script on the resume. You want to sound very natural and unscripted.

♦ Make the room behind you very clean and plain like an office environment would be. It should never look like you're filming from home. A solid color behind you is always a nice backdrop.

♦ Be patient; go through as many takes as you need to get it right. You can always edit segments later.

♦ Decide if you are you more comfortable sitting or standing.

♦ Relax and talk directly into the camera. Have someone stand directly behind the camera for you to look at if that makes you more comfortable.

♦ Make sure that the lighting is correct for you to be able to be seen clearly. You want your face to be adequately lit and you do not want any shadows, etc.

♦ Introduce yourself and briefly describe your resume. Be very brief! Your DVD resume should never be longer than a few minutes. You do not want someone to get bored and turn it off. You may mention just one or two previous employment choices as well as your education and any awards you have received.

♦ You can place the awards you have received as text on your DVD resume if you choose.

- With a DVD resume you may want to show some of the visual design elements that you have created to display on your resume.

- Speak clearly and make sure that the sound is good on the microphone. Use the same tips for being aware of your speaking found in the interview chapter.

- You may want to edit your resume. Design a transition to put between clips if you want to make it flow better.

- You can choose to use music that is not too loud and has no lyrics for background. The music should only compliment you and not take away from what you are saying.

- Make sure to always end the resume with your contact information in writing.

- Label the outside of your resume with your name and contact info as well.

- Test it out! Are you impressed? If you are not, do it over again or don't use it.

Chapter 7

<u>Interviews</u>

It's all about getting the interview!
Here are some tips once you are finally there!

Ask yourself these very important questions to meet the employer's expectations:

- ✓ *Do I look like the right person for the job?*
- ✓ *Do I present myself like the right person for the job?*
- ✓ *Do I conduct myself like the right person for the job?*

I am going to tear down all of the misconception that you have heard about interviews. Remember, you choose your destiny almost totally here. Most people do not think that way about the interview but you actually have about 89% of the control over the entire outcome. This is taking into account that you have researched their company as well as looked at the qualifications for the position to determine the right fit in the beginning. Now, they have already viewed your resume so it's time to meet them in person and hit the grand slam!

<u>*Quick Tip!*</u>

People hire people that they like, even over how much experience they perceive that you have. Personality projection during an interview is a must and you have to relax to do that and enjoy the interview so your true self can come out!

Job search jitters!
-Fears and nervousness caused by not knowing what to expect when making job inquiries and answering interview questions.

The more you know about the interview process, the less jittery and anxious you will feel!

Different Types of Interviews

It is important that you understand the purpose of each different type of interview setting. Learn how to conduct yourself with each type and you will be more confident when you are faced with any type of interview setting!

The Telephone Interview

The telephone screening interview happens very often because employers like to save time by "weeding out" the bad applicants quickly with this type of interview through asking applicants a few main questions over the phone that pertain to the position. These can be make-or-break questions on their own because the questions are usually the most pertinent requirements to fill the position. This way their interview time is much more effective, interviewing only applicants that have all of the basic requirements to fill the position. Any time you are contacted by or are contacting a company by phone, keep your job search portfolio near you so that you can easily answer their questions. These interviews usually happen unexpectedly so be ready! There are many more tips about telephone interviews in the chapter on Job Search Tips.

The In-Person Screening Interview

This type of interview is not conducted by the decision maker. It is like a pre-interview to make sure the basic qualifications are met and get a feel of many of your personal and professional attributes and to again, (just like the telephone interview) begin to "weed out" applicants that are not acceptable to make another appointment for the second interview with the decision maker. Some companies have professional screeners just for this purpose such as someone in their HR department.

The Selection Interview

The final decision maker conducts this interview type. There may be numerous interviews and you may be asked back to have another interview with the same interviewer or other interviewers as the other applicants are "weeded out." Always present yourself to the best of your ability with each interviewer as if they each have the authority to hire. It's a nice way for the company to see how well you establish rapport with other interviewers and the opinions of the other interviewers will be important to the final outcome so treat each interviewer with respect and establish a great rapport with each one. Show them that you are comfortable in establishing working relationships with different types of people. Just like the "Peer Group" Interview, you are proving how well you "fit" into the existing organization.

The Work Sample Interview

This type of interview is fabulous for designers of all kinds to show their portfolios, as well as artists of any medium, models, etc., or it can be as simple as typing up a letter on the computer in business format for the interviewer to show that you know your stuff as a secretary, data processor, etc. This is also a great opportunity for anyone to show their sales skills by presenting their skills and talents in a manner that grasps and holds the interviewer's attention. Use this as your opportunity to wow them with your talents!

154

The Panel (Group) Interview

This type of interview consists of three or more people and it is usually a surprise that there are so many interviewers. This is why it is so important to make sure to always have extra resumes on hand so that you may give your resume to each interviewer before starting. Answer questions directly to the individual interviewer who asked it but also maintain eye contact with all interviewers in the room. Show your attention by looking each one in the eye. Sometimes it can make questioning less stressful for you as you can look at another interviewer when you are speaking to give yourself a breather moment but then take your eye quickly back to make sure that you are keeping your attention on the original interviewer asking the question. You can't look around when you are interviewing with one individual and for me, I am one of those people who have to keep moving even if it's just my eyes, so this type of interview does not need to be stressful. Take your time and show respect to each individual interviewer.

The Peer Group Interview

This interview is conducted by the actual people who you would be working with side by side, your peers in the field. You will want to show that you can get along with everyone in the room and that your personality and style will fit well with your future co-workers. They will most likely be relaxed because they are already established at the company but that is even more reason for you to relax and enjoy this interview. Remember, people want to work with someone that they can get along with and enjoy being in their company!

You will not want to sound too intimidating by using monotone language and big words that people have to look up for their definitions! You also don't want to appear less than the smarty you are, so my advice is to get a feel of the room before speaking too much and see how casual or stiff this new bunch of people are. Those few extra moments you give yourself will give you a better chance of quickly adjusting your attitude and style to be seen as the perfect person for the job!

The Luncheon Interview

In this type of interview, what you order can be just as important as what you wear! Think of it like this, they are trying to see how you are in social situations so make sure you are smiling at everyone you see and treat your waiter/waitress with respect. Okay, so I am not going to tell you what to order, I don't know what kinds of food you like but I will give you some great hints on what NOT to order! My grooming and finishing teacher used to tell us, never order hard tacos if you want to make a nice, refined impression because the ingredients inevitably get everywhere no matter how hard you try! (That was one of the tests we had to pass off on how to eat properly in the course. Not as easy as you may think!) I also tell people who ask me dating advice to never eat bagels and cream cheese with your date because trust me- you will not want to smile with all that cream cheese in your beautiful teeth! So try not to order those or anything else that sticks to or in-between your teeth on a luncheon interview so that you are free to smile at appropriate times.

Show that the meal is not that important, that you are more interested in what is happening with the interview. Good ways to do that are to take small; easy to chew bites, remember you will be the one who is intended to do most of the talking! If you order meats, cut three very small pieces at a time, put the knife down and then relax and eat them individually, that way you are making sure that you are not constantly cutting. You are taking your time to eat the three small pieces. Also, you should not be overly hungry, order something simple and quick to eat. It's okay to leave food on your plate, you're there for the interview and do not need to make food the priority.

The proper way to eat a roll, by the way, is not to cut it in half and butter it but it is proper to break the bread with your hands and then only butter a bite sized piece with your knife and place a small buttered piece into your mouth at a time. I tell you that because if the company wants you to be graceful socially, they will also know that you are not breaking the bread properly. Score points for yourself if you already knew the proper way to do that! I also don't recommend ordering spaghetti if it tends to get sloppy, but you can get past this by lifting a small amount of spaghetti noodles by your fork and then with your other hand holding the spoon. (You are using both hands for this) You will then twirl the noodles from your fork in your spoon, using the spoon as a backing to get the noodles in good formation before eating. That way it is clean and bite sized. Practice makes perfect on that one!

Don't be overly dramatic asking the wait staff for lots of condiments or commenting on how late they are in bringing you your entrée etc. Remember, they are watching how well you do socially! Be generous whenever tipping. I have a rule, I never go out unless I not only have enough money for the meal, but also enough for a decent tip! Now that you know a few tips, enjoy the interview and enjoy the meal!

The Stress interview

The stress interview can really catch you off guard. In this type of interview the interviewer is deliberately combative and offensive. They do not let up until you are sufficiently stressed. I had a stress interview once that was so awful that the guy was literally leaping across the table yelling at me for no reason! My experience is why I completely disagree with companies using this tactic for filling their open positions. No applicant deserves to be bullied, offended or pushed over their limit in any environment, especially when it is a deliberate act. Some companies feel that it is important to know how you will react under stress but this is usually not an actual situation that you would encounter in the work environment. I have never had a customer so mad that they were leaping towards me in anger. If you do get through an interview like this, congrats! You're cooler than the average cat and you deserve the job but think about working for the company long term, is it worth whatever tactics they deem necessary to throw at you? Are you going to be happy there?

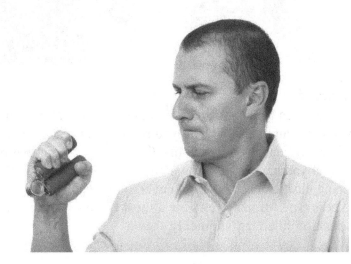

The Video Conference Interview

This type of interview can sometimes make job seekers nervous to be in front of the camera but I think it's a wonderful opportunity. Why would you not want to show them your fabulous personality and how great you look in your interview clothes? Don't worry about the camera thing; it can be your best friend second only to meeting in person! Companies sometimes interview this way to save money and time on traveling. Don't be a stiff on camera and you are golden! You may choose to use some of the tactics in the DVD resume section to help you do your best on camera. Relax in your own environment and have a great interview!

On The Spot Interview

There may be times when you are picking up an application and the interviewer suddenly asks for an interview with you right then. Of course you are going to oblige the interviewer because you would like the job! This is another reason why I tell you to make sure that you have your whole portfolio, resume, etc., with you even when picking up applications because you never know when this type of interview will happen. These types of interviews are almost always in your favor because usually they need the position filled rather quickly.

The Assembly Interview

Usually this interview type is designed to see who could be the best salesman, etc. Everyone that I have talked to who has gone through this type of interview says that it is very stressful because all of the other applicants are in the same room with you and they are all trying to answer the questions each better than the last applicant. There is usually a full room of people at this one. This is definitely an awkward interview, especially for people who are more shy or respectful of others. This type of interview works best for people who are louder than others and very comfortable standing out in the crowd. There is usually a second, more private interview for the chosen applicants following this interview.

The interviewing stage of your job search is critical. You can make or break your chance of being hired in the short amount of time it takes to be interviewed. Anyone can learn to interview well, and most mistakes can be anticipated and corrected before the interview.

Learn these hints & techniques to give you that winning edge!

Tips for acing that interview!

Do your research

If you research the company, you will know if you will be happy there, if you are qualified and meet their expectations, if you will reach your budget with their pay rate, if you look the part for that particular position, etc. Employers usually expect you to know a bit about their company and if you do not, you are an "I'll take ANY job" applicant. Most employers will not hire this type of applicant. They are not seen as loyal or personally motivated. You can better relax when you have made your decisions to be in that interview chair through sound research.

Practicing relaxation

Practice on your breathing and mentally allowing yourself to relax at the interview. There are many stress-reducing techniques used by public speakers that can certainly aid you in your interview process. Take a few slow, deep breaths before you go in for the interview. You will be able to relax and enjoy the interview much easier. The interviewer will take your cue and relax and feel comfortable with you as well which will definitely be a plus!

Always try to answer questions using more than one syllable words

The interview is a conversation setting and using one syllable responses can put the interviewer off and can also make you seem one dimensional or uninteresting. Arrogance is of course, another extreme and is absolutely out of the question as a trained interviewer will pick up on that immediately and again, you will appear one dimensional and will not be seen as a worthy candidate for consideration.

Don't keep talking!

Remember, the interview is a discussion forum and a chance that you have to highlight your skills to get the job! When our body is reacting to stress we can tend to over compensate while talking by telling too much information, which makes whatever you were trying not to highlight sound even worse or sound like you just talk too much. Try not to view the interview as you being interrogated. Instead, picture what it really is: You sitting at a table with one or more interviewers and answering their questions that they have to ask you as well as every other applicant and picture yourself being relaxed, witty, confident and sure of your abilities.

Make the first impression memorable

Make the first impression memorable and pleasurable for yourself and the interviewer. ***The first and last five minutes of any encounter will be remembered the most so make them count!*** Always leave on a positive note! Don't let your mind play tricks on your confidence. Remember, the interviewer is usually a manager who has been doing double the work load until the available position is filled so they need you just as much as you need them! Stop stressing!

Get the interviewer excited about you!

People love to hire individuals who are easy to get along with and excited about their company! Show how likeable and enthusiastic you are! You can be professional and demonstrate your interest and energy at the same time.

Check your posture before the interview

Stand tall and confident! This helps your own outlook and confidence and others perceive you as much more interesting and confident as well.

Review every type of appearance!

Review the way you look, how you behave, how you speak and how well you write. Each type of appearance is just as important as the rest. People make the original visual summation about you automatically in the first five seconds of meeting you, knowing this can be critical in your successful job search. It's not all just the visual however, you do need to master strong verbal communication skills which are highly valued by most employers. They are signs of educated and competent individuals.

Keep your collars tall

Mature job seekers can keep their collars taller to show less of the wrinkles we all get in the neck area as we age. This helps project a much younger, cleaner and more put together look.

Ask questions!

I've noticed that the best applicants will have questions for me. It is a nice change for the interviewer to know that you are interested in what they have to offer you as well! There are some great questions you could ask during an interview that you can view in this course. Having your own questions for the interviewer shows that you are comprehensive and that you have done your homework and that you are truly interested in the position.

Keep mints at the ready

Lots of people of any age have breath concerns due to oral issues. Make sure that hygiene won't be an interview issue. Don't forget the floss! Ask friends for honest opinions. We need to pay close attention to our oral hygiene because the saliva glands in the mouth stop producing as much as we age and makes a distinct odor, so keep mints in your pocket and mouth more often! Use mints before the interview. When you are actually in the interview however, you should have nothing in your mouth so you can speak clearly.

Ask for clarification

If you do not understand any particular one of the interview questions posed to you, it is perfectly acceptable to ask for clarification before giving an answer.

Don't have your piercings and tattoos visible

Facial piercings and tattoos that would be visible while wearing the work uniform are almost always seen as a negative! (Unless of course you are applying at a tattoo shop, in that case by all means show them off!) Whether you want to hear that or not, you will represent the owners of the company at which you are applying who are almost always more on the conservative side. I had an applicant who got through my interview very well but had a facial piercing and even though we pierced ears at that particular job, facial piercings were strictly not allowed by the company dress code. My hands were tied as an interviewer no matter how much I liked her or how qualified I considered her to be.

I asked the applicant if she would take it out while at work and she said "No because I just got it and paid $50.00 to get it done!" I was definitely not going to hire her after hearing that of course because it was against the company dress code but out of sheer curiosity, I told her she could be making a lot more money than fifty bucks if I hired her- (just to see how she would react) and she still wouldn't agree to take her piercing out during work hours. I felt sorry for that girl because she just cut her job prospects down considerably! Remember, you represent the company you work for and there are plenty of people who will gladly follow dress code standards in order to get the job! Don't limit yourself over something so trivial!

What are you really saying?

A trained interviewer will ask the same question a few different ways to monitor your "real response" This is a trick they use to get a feel for who you really are and be able to spot the red light responses. Be quick, sure and consistent about your answers to interview questions. Carefully review your positive statements before each interview and they will definitely be impressed with your responses!

Politeness and mannerisms

Do I really have to say it? Believe it or not, some people forget to pay attention to their basic mannerisms. You must be aware of yourself at all times and at the very least saying "please" and "thank you!" Your gestures and mannerisms should always be generally pleasant! If you go the extra mile here- compliment them, etc., you will be remembered as a person they would like to work with! It's well worth making this a priority to work on until it becomes an excellent habit! Do not discount the importance of politeness, good manners and excellent mannerisms.

Every negative must be answered with a positive!

Train yourself to respond positively to inquiries about your employment gaps and reasons for leaving, etc. This is explained in further detail in the course. Learn what your response to the hard questions should be before the interview. Whenever you need to account for something difficult, always end the sentence on a positive note! Place these answers that will help you in your data organizer sheets for each previous job. If you know how you will answer these hard questions with a positive end, you can relax!

Always dress one-up for the interview!

Once you have researched the company you should know how a person in the position you want is expected to dress every day at the job. Dress one level up from that. For instance, if you are expected to dress in very casual attire at work such as jeans and a t-shirt, you would wear a polo shirt and slacks to the interview. If you are expected to dress business casual (polo, slacks) then wear a button up shirt and very nice slacks for the interview. If you are expected to wear a button up shirt at work, wear a tie with it, etc. You need to look the part and the interview is always a special occasion to shine!

Practice interviews

Rehearse and practice interview questions before the interview, especially the hard questions! Prior to your interview, try to actually practice answering the different types of questions you may be asked. Even a simple question such as "Can you tell me about yourself?" can be surprisingly tough if you don't know how you might respond. The process of thinking each question through will help you feel less stressed and more prepared during the interview itself. Practice on turning anything negative into a positive and you will excel!

Quick Tip!

When doing a practice interview, make sure that you tell the interviewer what job you are applying for ahead of time so that when they play the part of interviewer, they can easier critique you on the way you are dressed, your qualifications, your wording, your resume etc. for what that particular job needs from an applicant.

Have a dress rehearsal before the interview!

Try everything on ahead of time! Have a friend or family member check the way you are dressed for that particular position and ask them if you look like the right person for the job. I recommend that you do that a day or two before the actual interview, not right before the time you need to leave in case something needs to be changed or fixed in any way. Wear clothes that are conservative for the interview, as well as clothes that are neat and clean. Do not wear anything too loud or attention grabbing. If you think that what you wear is not important- you should expect your job search to last much longer than the average person who is taking notice of themselves. Remember your shoes as well, to keep them in good condition and polished for the interview.

Remember your worth!

The main thing that I tell people who take my course is to remember that the interviewer needs to fill that position just as much as you need the job! You are not begging for the job in an interview setting, that is not what the interview is for, it is for seeing if there is a match between you and your skills and the job that they need to fill the open position for. Imagine yourself as the right person for the job and allow yourself to relax and have fun during your interview! This is a place where you can display your talents and please don't spare that great personality that is uniquely yours! Laugh a little! That may put you over the top as the interviewer is just another human being who is choosing someone that they would have to work with for the next few years as well! Don't be too stiff.

Why are you nervous?

"Logically, why am I nervous?" Ask yourself that question. You are not begging for employment, the employers are asking for people to fill their needs, and you are responding to their inquiry in order to fill your needs as well as theirs. It's as simple as that. The interview is simply a structured way to match the right people with the right employers. It is not always very formal either, depending on the company. Don't be too nervous, because if the worst happens, and they say you are not the right person for this position, would you ever want to work for someone who cannot see your worth or potential anyway?

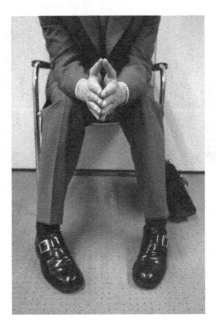

The employer needs you to be the right person!

Remember, the employer needs you to be the right person because they need to fill the position. They don't want to waste a lot of their precious time interviewing people! They can't afford that kind of time when there is already a hole in their staff to fill! The best interviewing candidates are usually confident and happy individuals. You don't ever see their desperation, (although they are a bit nervous.) They know that this one particular interview is not the only prospective position that they have in mind.

Quick Tip!

Have you ever gone on a blind date? Remember when you were sitting at the table trying to decide if you two were going to get along? Think of the interview as such a setting for a moment. How did you connect? What made this person someone you wanted to spend more or less time with? The interviewer wants to hire someone that they will get along with! They will likely have to spend a lot of time with the person that they choose to hire. Show your smile! Show your personality!

Keep your toes down!

When in the interview or even when waiting in the lobby area for the interview to begin, keep your toes down. Many people don't think about this but when you are sitting you can easily show the bottoms of your shoes and trust me that is one place on our outfit we would all rather not show off! You never know what the bottom of your shoes are going to look like.

Plan to be at the job for at least 5 years

Interviewers always plan to fill the open position for at least five years. If you don't plan to be there that long, let's look at that- exactly why did you apply there again? The interview question, "Where do you see yourself in five years?" is pretty standard. If you tell them somewhere else, or hesitate at all, the interviewer would rather overlook you because they will only have to go through the interview process again soon after all that job training and they feel that you are not committed. Interviewers don't have this kind of time to waste.

Rude interviewers

Caution! Do not try this trick unless you can really pull it off in a very subtle way! If you happen to get an interviewer or anyone else in the company who is very monotone, rude, and generally seems like they just don't like you, (which should be ultra-rare but we've all experienced them) you can use this old sales trick to turn around negative people. You would need to say only one sentence just at the same monotone level as they spoke to you and then gradually lift them by lifting your own voice tone. You can only do this if you start where they did though, (which is sometimes hard for nice people to do- that's okay, that's a good thing!) It's also a good trick to make them be more aware of themselves. If you pulled this trick off and the person is still very rude, do you really want to work every day with this person? Maybe there is a very good reason for this person needing to fill the position! Remember, there are other places to apply and you need to be happy at work or you will just end up looking for work again.

Transportation questions

Have transportation available and suggest in the interview that you would also utilize public transportation if your car ever needs to be serviced. You would not believe how many people would get the job if they had only agreed that if their car EVER fails that they are willing to take the bus! Don't have so much pride that you refuse because if you say "no"- the interviewer says "no" to you! It's that simple. They need to be able to depend on you no matter what happens!

Give a copy of your resume to each interviewer

Bring extra copies of your resume to the interview. If you are asked for another copy of your resume and you don't have one- that shows that you are unprepared. There are many times when you will have to interview with more than one person at the same appointment. Besides, you want everyone to have a copy of that fabulous resume right?

Quick Tip!

Have your coloring done by a professional, or buy a great book on the subject and do it yourself! Knowing what colors look great on you (And which ones - not so great) can have an enormous impact on how you feel and how you look. Sometimes wearing the wrong colors for your skin type, hair and eye color can even make you look like you are ill! At the same time, the right colors for you (Including clothing as well as makeup colors) can be an incredible asset to you for creating an amazingly polished and fresh appearance! There is a great book I recommend in the suggested reading portion of this book.
Allow your complimentary colors to highlight your best self!

Over-qualification, make it a plus not a minus!

If you've ever owned a business, or have previously been in management above the job level that you are currently looking for, these situations can be tricky. I have been in this situation many times and there was a time where I did not convince the interviewer adequately that I was trainable and was later sent a letter in the mail that I was not the right person for the job due to over-qualification. I analyzed what happened during the interview and there were a few problems with my presentation of myself. First was that my resume was not targeted correctly at the time, and I also did not convince the interviewer adequately that I could "settle" for the position as she put it. I really wanted the job but I needed to convince her that I was trainable and would take direction from her as a manager and I did not convince her of that to her satisfaction. These are the most important things to convince them of when you are over-qualified!

The interviewer has concerns of why you left in the first place and may have extra questions such as:
Are you too bossy?
Are you stubborn?
Are you intimidating?
Are you trainable?
Are you going to leave this job to start up your own business again?

In this situation, make sure that you express your love of teamwork and emphasize any previous experience with "assisting" your managers/co-workers as a team player. Your goal is to dispel any intimidation or skepticism the interviewer may have about your past experience and personality type.

Always analyze what you can do better in the interview and on your resume if over-qualification is a block to your progression.

Over-qualification for more mature individuals

Usually when I am troubleshooting the reasons why an older applicant is not getting the job it is due to over-qualification. I find that most are not aware of the intimidation that this may cause for the interviewer. Some may not even get to the interview stage until they "dumb down" their resume just a bit first. The interviewer may be younger and intimidated by the vast experience of the applicant. Also, the knowledge is very obviously superior due to the life experience of the older applicant and no one wants to hire someone who is more qualified than themselves for fear that their own job will be taken over! There are also many more of the transferable skills that come from having more life experience to take into consideration. Take this as a compliment!

It can be an easy fix but you do have to do some fast talking, letting the interviewer know that you are trainable and can easily take direction from others is very important! Show how your experience and wisdom has helped you and how it can help you and their company in the position you want. Let them know that you enjoy working with people of all ages and personality types. Show that you would fit well within the company and you should do great! Remember, this is not *your* issue, but it is an issue that you may find yourself answering to due to the insecurities of others.

Discover and review your interview weaknesses

Review your own personal weaknesses that are unique to you while in an interview setting. Everyone has them such as fidgeting, saying "umm" a lot, talking nervously etc. You can discover them easily just by role playing with someone you know and having them ask you some interview questions. Make an effort to master them!

Tell the interviewer that the job is right for you

Let the potential employer know why you think it would be a good job for you. For instance, if you shop there and you happen to love the store already, they would like to hear it! Plus that tells them that you can sell their products well because you already believe in them! A good interviewer should ask you why you would be applying there. For me this is a great searching question. Go ahead and let them know you want the job and why!

Translate your skills into what they can understand

When you research the company, focus on what their needs are and how you can fill their needs with your particular skills. At the interview, customize your answers as much as possible in terms of the needs of the employer.

You've got skills!

Show what you can do for their company! Present yourself as someone who can really add value to an organization. Talk about your skills that can be valuable to the company's needs. All transferable skills are valuable to the employer in one form or another- that is how important they are! Let them know! If you don't, no one else will! Life skills are priceless. Remind yourself of your own personal transferable skills and get ready to excite the interviewer!

Show that you can fit into the existing work environment

Some transferable skills are very important when letting a potential employer know that you will fit into their organization, especially when it comes to getting along with work associates who are already there. Employers need to select someone who has the right skills but who can also fit well as far as their personality. Choose at least two words from the self-management skills checklist that show how well you get along with others and let them know!

Give specific stories

Whenever you let an interviewer know about your skills, it is more memorable to them when you tell of a specific instance in the past where you have had to utilize that particular skill. The added benefit is that you will be more believable and they can picture how they might need that skill in the same types of circumstances in their work environment. Past performance is the best indicator of future performance!

Take a moment

Take a breath whenever you need. Taking a moment to frame your answers will allow you to more confidently answer them! There is nothing wrong with slowing yourself down for a moment. You can use words and terms that help you buy time such as: Good question, well, sometimes, etc. Just remember, "umm" and "uhh" are not words! They do not go over well at the interview. Be aware of yourself and take the time to speak clearly.

Don't badmouth former employers!

Never *EVER* talk bad about your previous manager or fellow work associates! This just makes the interviewer uneasy as they think that you will have the same attitude about them when you leave that job. Trust me, the more you say someone else was the problem, the more you are perceived to be the one with the problem! Whenever I have an applicant who is talking badly about a former employer, I actually listen as if they are talking directly about me because I know that they will probably be saying the same exact things about me when they leave my company! This is how directly it can apply. Be positive!

Smile and get the interviewer excited about you!

Use your natural charm and let them know in a humble but direct way that you would be an excellent individual to work with!

Thank the interviewer for their time

The interviewer has taken out valuable time to meet with you. Valuable time away from doing their regular job, plus usually they are doing extra work until the available position is filled so if you acknowledge that you know that their time is valuable, it will be well received and very appreciated.

Simple pleasantries are too often overlooked especially if you are nervous but these simple things can put you over the top and Get you remembered!

Reintroduce yourself whenever calling back

When calling back a prospective employer, introduce yourself again and explain why you are calling. So many people expect the interviewer to know them by name. Chances are they've probably interviewed at least five people other than you. Making assumptions like that will just make you seem slightly annoying.

Do not call back the interviewer more than once

It is not necessary to continually try to contact the employer to see if you've got the job unless they specifically tell you to do so. You should however, always contact them once after the interview via letter, e-mail or phone call to thank them for their time and let them know that you are still interested in the position.

I remember a few different times where I had interviewed applicants who were just as qualified as the others that I had interviewed but, then some would actually call me daily which is highly inappropriate. Some even called more than that if I were in meetings etc., and leave numerous messages. I had one who called me three times a day! This became very frustrating as most employers don't have time to keep talking to potential applicants. The ones who got the job were the ones that weren't so desperate that they had to continually call and interrupt my work day.

Many times an employer will *not* let you know if you *haven't* got the job, so bugging them won't help you, just keep on your job search until a job offer is made that you choose to accept. No problem, you're at your next interview with the next prospective company anyway- right?

Always give your two weeks' notice!

The best time to find a new job is when you still have a job. To have a job already and to give two weeks' notice will look very enticing to the interviewer as they expect that you will give them the same respect when you leave that position.

Always evaluate each interview

- ♦ What do you think went well in the interview?
- ♦ How can you improve for the next interview?
- ♦ Did you present yourself with confidence?
- ♦ What can you clarify in your resume better?
- ♦ What questions did I not answer in the best way I could have?
- ♦ What questions did I answer in the best possible way?
  (Write those fabulous answers down for the next one!)

When evaluated correctly, what happened at the last interview may make all the difference in making sure that the next one is much more successful!

Don't be afraid to admit mistakes and challenges!

Employers know that no one is perfect and they would like to know what your challenges are before they hire you. You need to have a great answer for questions like "What is your greatest challenge" and it is asked in many different ways. This does not have to scare you- just make sure to always end the negative with a positive.

Also, you can choose the negative traits you have that may actually be a positive for their line of work, such as "I am a perfectionist," or "I am a clean freak" etc. Give specific examples on how you have turned negatives into positive traits. Honesty is a bigger plus than you may think! Some negative traits, like these examples can actually be good for the employer so go ahead and let them know your challenges, just keep them in the most positive sense, everyone has challenges!

Think of a positive answer that you will give to the question "Give me an example of a mistake you have made at work." Always know what you're going to say! Tell them the mistake, but always say how you learned from it or what you did to make the situation better. These questions do not need to blindside you- just think it over beforehand!

Excellent Body Language!

REMEMBER!
Non-verbal clues start as soon as you enter the building!

♦ Turn off cell phones before entering the company.

♦ Make eye contact! This is essential human contact as well as it helps you seem much more honest.

♦ Don't lean back and slump in your chair. This can make you seem too relaxed, frumpy, not sincere or even arrogant.

♦ Keep those hands out of your pockets! Be open with your body language. You do not want to play with coins, keys, etc. in your pockets.

♦ Do not clench or wring your hands. This shows agitation or that you are subconsciously trying to console yourself about something.

♦ Do not tap your pen or pencil.

♦ When you place your hands in front of your lips when speaking, you are usually indicating that this particular subject is not something that you would like to comment on or talk about. Keep your hands on a notebook or pen if you need to.

♦ Pay attention to the sighs in the conversation as well, this can comprise too much of the non-verbal communication.

♦ Do not chew on gum, pencils, etc. Nothing should be in your mouth while speaking to the interviewer.

♦ Wearing your smile is the best accessory you can possibly have. A genuine smile can relax you as well as the interviewer and will be incredible for building your confidence!

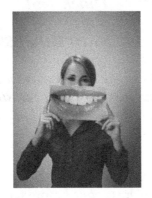

♦ Sitting closer can make you seem alert and motivated, leave enough space for the interviewer to be comfortable with their personal space (usually 3 ft. or so) and you are doing great!

♦ Keep your focus on the interviewer. Relax and lean slightly forward to look interested in the interviewer. A great tip is to sit with your bottom at the back of the chair and lean forward slightly. This helps promote good posture as well as showing interest.

♦ Do not fiddle with your jewelry.

♦ Do not get distracted by people, surroundings, or even the clock. This can make you seem like someone who will not focus on work tasks or business at hand.

♦ Do not sit with your arms crossed, this is a gesture that can make you seem angry, defensive or agitated.

Office Attire Dos and Don'ts

DO!

♦ Always check the company dress code before having to get talked to by your supervisor! The office is usually a more conservative environment than most any other place.

♦ Wear skirts at a modest length (Just above the knee or longer.)

♦ Wear button up shirts. This can make you look more refined.

♦ Wear shirts with collars.

♦ Jackets are always great, especially ones with great shoulders. They give you a more credible, authoritative, competent and approachable look.

♦ Wear shoes that are not open toed, they are more appropriate for the work environment.

♦ Pay attention to your shoes. Keep them shined and in good condition.

♦ Pay attention to the fit of your clothing. Poor fit can make you look frumpy.

♦ Pay attention to your grooming; make sure that makeup and hair are always polished.

♦ Beards and mustaches only work when always kept neatly trimmed. If you can't find the time to keep up with the trimming, lose the facial hair! If you can keep it trimmed, it can be a very nice accessory to your look!

♦ Ensure nicely pressed, clean and neat items. Never neglect the cleanliness and condition of your clothing.

♦ Wear fabulous high heels. They are definitely power items in your work wardrobe but if you are wearing heels that are far too high for you it will not give the effect of power but just the look of a little girl playing dress-up, and not being able to walk correctly just translates to instability. You're going for the look of stability and power!

♦ Purchase quality fabrics. They are worth the extra money up front. Try to stay away from fabrics that can make you look more run down, frumpy and even incompetent. Take your time to try on many types of business attire before making a purchase. You won't need to go out and buy a whole new wardrobe. It's much better to have a few good quality items that you can mix and match than to have many items that are not the best quality!

♦ Wear modest clothing, giving more credit to your competence at work rather than calling attention to your body.

Quick Tip!

Go through your work wardrobe on weekends and iron, mend etc. to make sure that everything is always ready-to-wear! If you don't prepare properly, you can be running late, trying to hurry and you pull out a jacket and oops! You forgot to mend that button! My personal rule is I can't hang it up if it is not ready-to-wear so I always know if it needs ironing etc.

♦ Pay attention to your hygiene, oral and otherwise before someone else notices!

STEP IT UP!

Following these guidelines are incredible for building confidence! You will impress yourself first, before anyone else and knowing that you are looking smart and competent will make your confidence absolutely soar!

There are different types of business dress standards for each company. Some of these are: casual, business casual, business, formal business. No matter how casual the office attire is, NEVER dress in the "don't" category!

DON'T WEAR! (Unless the job requires you to do so!)

- Sweat pants

- Hats

- T-shirts

- Jeans with tears in them (Most companies do not allow jeans all together)

- Tank tops

- Sneakers, flip flops or sandals

- Spaghetti straps

- Strapless tops

- Shorts

- Short skirts

- Body piercings

- Items that show the stomach area

- Items that are too dramatic or flashy in the office environment.

- Anything too sloppy, pay attention to the fit as well, making sure that the items are not too large, which can make even a nice suit look sloppy!

- Anything too tight. Clingy knits and tight clothing can look quite immodest when the fit is too tight.

- Shirts that have writing on them, you are not a walking billboard or comedy show at work.

- Too much perfume. You do need to smell nice but too much perfume can be overpowering and you never know which of your coworkers or customers may have serious allergies.

♦ Clothing with "deconstruction" elements, meaning clothing that looks deliberately torn apart, fringe, holes or ripping, seaming inside out, wear marks, etc. Even if these items are trendy at the time, they should never be used in the office.

♦ Clothing that reveal anything that you are insecure about. You should always dress to highlight the positive and don't worry about the negative, cover that up. If you are insecure about a scar, your legs, your ankles? Don't wear a skirt- wear pants! If you are insecure about a tummy, wear a jacket that hits you right in the middle of it. Do not go too high or too low. You can camouflage just about anything that you consider a flaw!

Quick Tip!

Install a full length mirror close to the door so that you may take a look at yourself right before you leave the house. You may save yourself some embarrassment later! The outfit you've chosen may be perfect but the addition of your breakfast you spilled on it and did not notice, well, may not be the best look! You can also use it to give yourself some confidence as well. Do you look the part for this position? Very nice! Go for it!

Stand Taller! You will feel better about yourself and you will see the difference in the confidence you will have immediately!

Quick Tip!

We need to stop worrying so much about what we are going to say to employers during job interviews, initial contacts, etc. and make sure to pay attention to the visual details of our presence. This next section is very clear on why it is so important to be very aware of our visual projection and body language!

How we are perceived by others is based on:

55% Visual Clues

38% Tone of voice

7% What we say

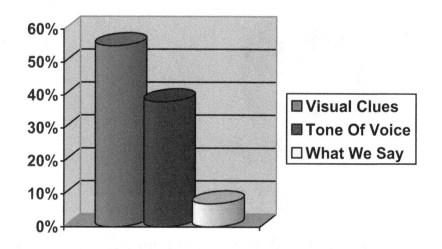

Lorna Kibby from Leadership Solutions says:
The studies that reveal the way we understand common everyday messages communicated to us are shocking! Experts agree that only 7 percent of our comprehension is based on the actual words a person uses; 38% is based on tone of voice. That leaves a whopping 55% of our comprehension that comes straight from what we see when we communicate.

Body language experts around the world agree that our visual clues are what can make or break a chance at acing the interview!

Remember, your body language needs to be confident!
Shake hands firmly, smile and look the interviewer in the eyes.

How to Answer Interview Questions

➢ *Always give an honest answer.*
➢ *Any time you have to say something that can be viewed as negative, always*
  follow it with a positive statement.
➢ *Never complain, whine about, or backstab your former employer.*
➢ *PRACTICE your answers ahead of time!*
➢ *Relax and allow your answers to flow smoothly.*

Tell me about yourself:
>   Don't share personal details unless they relate to the job. This question can inspire you
>   to tell them personal details such as how you are married, that you have two kids, a
>   dog, etc. but that's not what they want to hear. Concentrate on telling the employers
>   how you would be a good fit for their job by telling them more about your work-self
>   like "I am a very self-motivated and cooperative individual," etc.

What is your ideal job?
>   Give an all-purpose, general answer like, "My ideal job is a place where I can be
>   successful and improve my skills," or "A job where I can utilize my skills and where I
>   am appreciated for my work ethic."

Why have you changed jobs so often?
or Why haven't you had any other jobs?

Employers want workers who are dependable, stable, and know how to work hard. They need a good explanation for what may look like job hopping or job stagnation. They can understand answers like: "I haven't had a job before because I was concentrating on school." "It was a seasonal job." "I found out that I didn't like that kind of work. But, it helped me figure out what kind of work I do like." "The company went out of business." "I worked there a long time because the work was satisfying and my coworkers were wonderful."

What is your best quality?

If you can't say something good about yourself, why should anybody else? This is not a time to be modest, but don't be boastful. Be honest. Choose one of your good qualities that would be beneficial to an employer. "I do a high quality job." "I am dependable and honest."

What is your greatest weakness?

Everyone has weaknesses. You will not be believed if you say you have none, or can't think of any. The employer may think you do not have a realistic view of yourself and may not be able to see a reason to improve yourself, so be prepared to share your weakness, especially one that will be non-threatening to the employer. As soon as you share that weakness, tell how you are overcoming that weakness. For example: "I lose my temper easily. But I know that isn't right, so I practice techniques such as walking away until I can calmly discuss the problem. I find that when I have time to think it through, I can come up with a constructive solution that is fair to everyone."

Give me two reasons why I should hire you.

Interviewers want to hear words like: loyal, initiative, team player, hard worker, get along with teachers (that translates in their ears to supervisor), quick learner, dependable, etc. Be honest!

What do you think is fair to expect from a job?

Be honest but don't make it sound like money is your number one priority. Don't make it sound like you are after someone else's job. Good answers could be: "I like to be treated with respect," or "I like to feel appreciated for my hard work."

Interview Questions

These are samples that you may or may not choose to use just for discussion purposes

DRE'S Example Q&A

There are questions that you should ideally ask the interviewer- they are labeled "Your Q".

YOUR Q: What else can I tell you that will convince you that I'M the right person for this job?

Use this question as an ANSWER to questions as well- it's just as effective! I personally love it when someone asks me this one- use it! If you know you're qualified-- why not? You will stand out- I promise! You have nothing to lose but the job you really want! Make sure your tone of voice doesn't have a hint of arrogance or it can have the exact opposite effect of what you want. Smile and ask this one!

188

Q: Why are you applying for this job?

A: I would like a field change where I can utilize my computer skills. (Replace the word computer with the skill of your choice)

Q: How do you spend your free time?

A: I love to shop, I have a lot of friends that I socialize with, I enjoy spending time with my family, and I like to take short classes on things I am interested in- which are many!

Quick Tip!

Employers want to know you have a life outside of work! They like employees who have ways of releasing their stress after work. When asked about how you spend your free time, go ahead and tell them about your fun self in 30 seconds or less- don't hold back here! You may also find a common interest you have!

Q: Are you willing to relocate?

A: I like the area that I am in however, that would be something I would be willing to consider. (Managers & some Assistant Manager positions will usually require a willing answer.)

Q: Why are you leaving your present job?

A: I would like to work in a field that interests me and where I can use the experience that I have to better challenge me. (This answer applies to your transferable experience as well)

Q: Why have you changed jobs so frequently?

A: Go ahead and let them know that you have had some interest in other careers and that you have learned a lot of different skill sets from each previous position but also reassure them that you know exactly what you want now.

YOUR Q: What type of training would I receive as a result of obtaining this position?

Q: Why should I hire you over anyone else?

A: I know I am capable of doing the job right. My experience has taught me things I could not learn from a book or any other type of training. The people skills I have can only be taught through experience.

Q: Where are you at in life?

A: I am ready to take on new and exciting challenges!

Quick Tip!

Be slightly vague if you are unsure of what they are asking for in a "searching" question. They can always re-ask you in a different form if they aren't satisfied with the answer you gave them. By then, you know what they want which is definitely to your advantage!

Q: Why shouldn't I hire you?

(Ooh! Tough one! Here's how I handled it- think positive end!)

A: I am a perfectionist so I am not very good to myself when I have something before me that needs to get done. I don't rely on anyone else to help me; I take the task on myself. I don't work until I am done; I work until the job is done! (That works for them- for a few reasons: That statement said that I am self-motivated, I will make sure the job is done right because of my own "perfectionist standards," I am not putting the work on others, so I am the person who gets the job done whether I'm being helped or not.)

Q: What is your greatest accomplishment?

A: I had a child and lived through the labor! (Yes, you can still be professional and have a sense of humor! If you are naturally funny, but not over the top or inappropriate in any way, you can really be seen as a great person to work with- so loosen up!)

Q: What is your most serious problem?

A: I ask a lot of questions, I like to know everything about what I am doing and the "why's" behind it so that I can better understand the process and do it right! (The negative Q is turned into a positive A!)

Q: Describe the ideal job for you.

A: Working with a company where I can expand, (Has opportunities for advancement) utilize my skills, and having fun at my job. (Vague enough to use at most any interview but precise as well.)

Q: How long have you been looking for a job?

A: The answer should most always be that you just started! If not, be prepared to make an account as to why it has taken you so long to find a job. You don't need to go there!

Q: Are there any other job offers that you have had?

A: Be honest! Do not try to impress them by saying yes, you may just have to answer the next questions, "Oh really? What companies have given you the offers?" and "Why have you not accepted these offers?" etc. Yikes! Do you really want to go there? Simply saying, "No, I have just started looking" is very acceptable and a much less sticky answer!

Q: Describe how your education fits into this position.

A: I am proficient in various types of software and because of that I can easily learn any new program that is placed before me. (You can also use this question to show off your favorite transferable skills!)

Q: What would you do if you became bored at work?

A: (This one should be easy for anyone with a good work ethic!) I don't allow myself to get bored I like to keep moving so I start cleaning and taking care of the equipment around me through dusting the office, etc. I like to work in a clean environment. I also enjoy interacting with the customers and asking them if there is anything that they need and how I might be able to assist them in finding what they need.

Q: What skills are you bringing to this position?

A: I am proficient in various software applications, including operating systems. I am ready to take on new and exciting challenges! (Again, you can also use this question to show off your favorite transferable skills!)

HOW WILL *YOU* SELL IT?

Sometimes interviewers like to point to something simple in the room such as a box of tissues and ask you to sell it to them. I have had this question fired at me before and it caught me off guard although it's very standard. This could be anything in the room; the point is that you need to sell it to them. This is an on the spot question so be ready for it. Think beforehand how you might sell something that might be in the room next to you right now. What can you tell them about this product that may be of worth to them? How would you persuade them to want to actually make the purchase? This on the spot question is designed to see how you can sell a product in a pinch and how you react under pressure.

I don't necessarily agree with this type of questioning because in the real world you would probably not sell an item unless you know something about the item and the consumer first however, if that is the question you get- sell it, sell it, sell it! If you don't know the specifics of a product make it up as you go such as: "This is the leading product in the industry," etc. You don't know that for sure but then again, you were asked to sell something you know nothing about. Don't fret; just answer the question by confidently selling it so that you can move on to the next question. Work on how you might sell it in as few words as possible so that you end the sale quick.

Too many people do not do well on this question because they continue on and on about the product. Some suggest that you ask questions of the interviewer like a salesman would to figure out the needs of the customer before trying to sell it to them. I don't agree with that at all- the interviewer does not want to turn this quick question into a ten minute bore! Just sell the item to them on its own merits and get on with the interview questioning.

Q: Where do you see yourself in five years?

A: (The same answer to the "Describe the ideal job for you" question is excellent!) Working with a company where I can expand, (Has opportunities for advancement) utilizing my skills, and having fun at my job. (Vague enough to use at most any job but precise as well.) You don't want to get very personal here- employers looking to fill a manager position do not want to hear about how a female applicant may want to have a baby soon because that brings up maternity leave. They have to find a replacement for you or you may leave the job all together. They want to hire someone that will be able to work the job for at least five years. Otherwise, they may as well not waste their time on hiring you and they will keep searching for someone who will appear more work-stable. If having children soon is one of your goals, great- but it would be wise to keep your answers to these types of questions as job-oriented as possible if you want the job!

Quick Tip!

BRING IT ON!

Welcome the tough questions! If you know how you will answer them in a positive manner, those tough questions lose their intimidation! I would like you to get to a point where you can actually hope that you get the tough ones because you will be the one applicant who is ready and not blind-sided by them. You will definitely stand out! Turn them into a positive and you are self-assured every time! Make it your goal to master them in your practice interviews.

Q: Describe your former co-workers personalities.

A: Don't go off on what a gossip one girl was and what a jerk one guy was and so on, this question is designed to see how you really related to them and how it "really was". This "searching" question can be answered in the best way by being positive about everyone.

Now it's your turn!

Look at the basic interview questions on the next few pages and answer them individually in context to your own situation.

Interview Questions

Familiarize yourself with each question and create an answer that you are comfortable with saying in an interview setting. The answer should flow smoothly.

General questions:
- ➢ *How can I help you today?*
- ➢ *What position are you applying for?*
- ➢ *How did you learn about this position?*
- ➢ *What do you like about our product(s)?*
- ➢ *What type of work interests you?*
- ➢ *What qualities do you think are necessary to be successful in this kind of work?*
- ➢ *What do you think might be some of the disadvantages of this kind of work?*
- ➢ *Why are you returning to work after so long?*

Questions regarding money and benefits:
- ➢ *What was your salary for your last job?*
- ➢ *Would you be willing to take a pay cut to get this job?*
- ➢ *What benefits are most important to you?*
- ➢ *What benefits did you receive from your previous employer?*

Questions regarding education:
- ➢ *Did you graduate high school? or Do you have the equivalent?*
- ➢ *Why did you choose your particular major in college?*
- ➢ *Why did you leave college before graduating?*
- ➢ *Why are you not applying for a field that you majored in?*
- ➢ *What brought your grades down in school?*
- ➢ *What subjects did you enjoy?*
- ➢ *What made you choose your major/minor?*
- ➢ *What subjects did you find challenging?*
- ➢ *What were your extracurricular activities?*
- ➢ *What types of books have you read?*

Questions regarding training:

➢ *Have you had any special training?*
➢ *Would you prefer a formal training program or on the job training?*
➢ *What types of machines do you know how to operate?*
➢ *What type of job-related experience have you acquired while you were in the military?*
➢ *What type of training do you have that might be helpful to this company?*

Questions regarding availability:

➢ *What hours are you available for work?*
➢ *Can you work a full time shift?*
➢ *Can you work part time?*
➢ *What shift would you prefer?*
➢ *Can you work other shifts besides your preference(s)?*
➢ *Would your schedule allow you to trade off working both morning and afternoon shifts in an average work week?*
➢ *Can you work the graveyard shift?*
➢ *Can you work weekends?*
➢ *Are you willing to work overtime?*
➢ *We rotate shifts every three months, would this be acceptable to you?*

Questions regarding transportation:

➢ *Is your driver's license current?*
➢ *What type of transportation do you have?*
➢ *Can you travel considerably?*
➢ *Would you be able to relocate?*
➢ *Do you have preferences on where you would like to relocate?*
➢ *Do you have any experience driving company vehicles?*
➢ *Would you be willing to use public transportation to get to work if necessary?*

Questions regarding your future plans:

> ➤ *How does this position fit with your overall career goals?*
> ➤ *What other positions have you considered applying for?*
> ➤ *How long would you stay with the company if you were offered this job?*
> ➤ *What would you like to be doing five years from now? Ten years from now?*
> ➤ *Where would you prefer to live? Why?*
> ➤ *Do you plan to go back to school someday?*
> ➤ *Where are you at in life?*

Questions regarding your employment experience:

- *What experience are you bringing to the position?*
- *What other jobs have you held?*
- *What did you like most about your last job?*
- *What did you like the least about your last job?*
- *How do you know that you can perform the tasks for this position?*
- *What do you know about this particular position?*
- *What do you know about our company?*
- *Are you good at multitasking?*
- *Do you get along well with people?*
- *Have you ever had trouble with other people on the job?*
- *Describe a time where you had a challenging customer or other work situation and how you handled it.*
- *Can you take criticism well?*
- *What would you do if you had a personality clash with a supervisor?*
- *What would you do if you started to become bored with work?*
- *What if a personal problem interfered with your performance?*
- *How would you rate your ability to follow instructions?*
- *Will you fight to get ahead?*
- *Do you prefer to work alone or with others?*
- *Can you list any examples of your creativity?*
- *What supervisory or leadership roles have you held?*
- *How motivated are you?*
- *What have you learned from previous jobs?*
- *What do you think determines a person's progress in a good company?*
- *What have you done to show your willingness to work?*
- *What qualifications do you have for this position?*
- *Do you believe you would be successful in this position? Why?*
- *How did you become interested in this type of work?*
- *Are you a good manager?*
- *Can you work well under pressure?*
- *Would you mind if I contact your current employer?*
- *Why do you believe that you are a good manager?*
- *Would your last employer recommend you?*
- *Have you ever helped to reduce operating costs? How?*
- *Have you had experience hiring people before? What do you expect of an employee?*
- *Have you ever fired anyone? How did you handle the situation?*
- *Have you ever developed or helped to develop any programs? What kind? How?*
- *Do you enjoy routine work?*
- *If I asked your former employer about you, what would they likely say?*
- *What was your most important accomplishment during your school years?*
- *What did you learn from part-time or summer job experiences?*
- *Have you ever worked on a volunteer basis?*
- *Do you have references?*
- *Tell me about the other places you have worked.*

Common problem interview questions:

- ➤ *Tell me a little about yourself.*
- ➤ *What is the best decision you have ever made?*
- ➤ *What is the worst decision you have ever made?*
- ➤ *Why have you had so many jobs?*
- ➤ *How long have you been looking for a job?*
- ➤ *Have you had any other job offers? From what company? At what salary?*
- ➤ *Are there other fields that you are interested in?*
- ➤ *What do you consider to be a major weakness of yours?*
- ➤ *What is your greatest accomplishment?*
- ➤ *If you could change anything about yourself what would that be?*
- ➤ *What is your greatest challenge?*
- ➤ *What amount of salary do you require?*
- ➤ *Why do you have this gap in your job history?*
- ➤ *What is your philosophy of life?*
- ➤ *How would you describe your personality?*
- ➤ *How would your co-workers describe you?*
- ➤ *How would your friends describe you?*
- ➤ *Why do you want to work for this company?*
- ➤ *Why did you leave your former position?*
- ➤ *What does failure mean to you?*
- ➤ *Where do you see yourself in five years?*
- ➤ *What do you like to do in your free time?*
- ➤ *Why should I hire you over anyone else?*
- ➤ *What kind of job are you looking for?*
- ➤ *Have you had any experience in this type of position?*
- ➤ *What is the worst challenge that you still currently have to deal with about yourself?*

Quick Tip!

Use these questions when you conduct your practice interviews! Make sure that you study these questions and get to know exactly how you will answer each of them in a positive manner. Become comfortable with how you will answer each of these interview questions whenever you are asked.

Questions to ask the employer during the interview!

- ➤ *How many employees work for this organization?*
- ➤ *How did you first become interested in this business?*
- ➤ *How long has this position been available?*
- ➤ *Would I be able to speak with the person who held this position previously?*
- ➤ *Is relocating an option? Is it a requirement?*
- ➤ *What is the next step in the decision-making process?*
- ➤ *When will a decision be made about this position?*
- ➤ *What are the responsibilities and accountabilities of this position?*
- ➤ *What are the important areas for future development in this industry?*
- ➤ *What personal qualities are necessary to succeed in this kind of business?*
- ➤ *Are there individuals within the company who may be qualified for the position?*
- ➤ *Is a written job description available?*
- ➤ *Where would I be working?*
- ➤ *How many people will be reporting to me?*
- ➤ *What type of software will I be expected to use?*
- ➤ *Who owns the company?*
- ➤ *What does the company consider unique about itself?*
- ➤ *Would it be possible to arrange a tour of your facilities?*
- ➤ *Could you tell me a little about the people with whom I would be working most closely?*
- ➤ *Would you recommend this profession to a person considering it for a career?*
- ➤ *What can someone do to get a head start in learning to be a (n) _____?*
- ➤ *Could you describe a typical day in this position?*
- ➤ *What do you like the most about your profession?*
- ➤ *What do you most dislike about your profession?*
- ➤ *What are some typical daily pressures of managing this sort of business?*
- ➤ *What are the company's short and long range objectives?*
- ➤ *Before you are able to make a decision to hire, how many interviews should I expect to go through and with whom?*
- ➤ *How did this position become available? Was the previous person promoted? If so, what is their title now?*
- ➤ *As you think about the position, what aspects of this job would you like to see performed better?*
- ➤ *Does this job usually lead to other positions within the company? Which ones?*
- ➤ *What are the common qualities in your successful employees?*
- ➤ *What do you like best about this company?*
- ➤ *Do new employees in this position generally receive on-the-job training or formal training?*
- ➤ *What else can I tell you to convince you that I am the right person for the job?*

REASONS FOR LEAVING

I QUIT!

When stating why you left a job, it is important to avoid using the words "I was fired", "I quit," "I was terminated," or "For personal reasons." These responses may reduce your chances of being hired. Always look for positive statements to use when answering this question. If you respond with, "Will explain at the interview," you will be called on to do so! (If you are offered an interview in the first place after giving that answer!) Often there are much better ways to respond.

You can say "I resigned" rather than saying "I quit" or something equivalent that is a little less harsh sounding. Never say for "Personal Reasons" as they will wonder what you are trying to hide from them. This does not project an honest personality right up front and they will instinctively not hire the person who isn't upfront with them during the interview.

I WAS LAID OFF!

Being laid off of your job is not a negative reason for leaving. Lay-offs happen quite a bit in the work force. If you were laid off from a job due to no fault of your own, go ahead and tell the interviewer the circumstances of the lay-off. This is never anything to be ashamed of.

Phrases you might want to use for being laid off from a company include: lack of work, lack of operating funds, temporary employment, seasonal employment, company closed, plant closing, company downsized, corporate merger, etc.

I WAS FIRED!

BUT WHAT IF I WAS FIRED?

You were fired? Just be honest! Yes I said it! As long as you can state what happened and how you have learned from it- (and here's the kicker) without bad mouthing the previous employer, you may be surprised to find that most interviewers will understand! Think about it, chances are the interviewer has probably been in that same position before and therefore will understand the situation and appreciate your honesty.

I have hired more than one applicant just for the mere fact that they were honest with me about being fired or owning up to their challenges. I knew that they were not afraid to own up to their challenges and they have learned hard lessons from their experience. I also decided that an honest employee is better than someone who can blow smoke well! My sincere advice is to be honest- but also always be positive with all aspects of the situation!

FIRED

HERE'S HOW YOU CAN GET THROUGH IT!

1. *Be honest! But use better wording- Instead of saying "I was fired," or "I was terminated," you can say "I was let go" (See how it takes the edge off a bit?) There are terms that sound very harsh and some that sound a little more forgiving. Also, depending on the circumstances, you may want to rethink your wording for why you were let go in the first place- again, be honest but take the edge off by wording it better! Think this through well and you will not be so afraid of this coming up!*

2. *Show the interviewer that you are not afraid of the question. The more you say it out loud in practice interviews the easier it is to be confident saying it when it counts.*

3. *State what happened calmly and do not bad mouth your former employer or coworkers during the discussion!*

4. *Tell what you have learned from the experience and how you are excited to apply what you have learned at the next job opportunity!*

5. *Don't dwell on it, move along with the question quickly, it is what it is, you don't have to go on about it, which just makes it sound worse than it really is.*

6. *Stay confident! This question is not as scary as you may think it is, many people have been fired at least once in their lives, it can happen to the best of us. Just remember how you have learned from the experience and stay focused on the person you are now rather than any past failures.*

Negative reasons for leaving your former job

- The pay was too low.
- I was fired.
- I was terminated.
- For personal reasons.
- I had problems with the boss.
- I had problems with co-workers.
- I quit.
- I was arrested.
- The work was too hard.
- The job was too dirty.
- I was dealing with too much responsibility.

Positive Reasons for leaving your former job

- I desire a career-oriented position in ___(field in which you are applying).
- I had an opportunity for a better job.
- Lack of work within the company.
- I desired a more challenging position.
- I wanted a position with responsibility.
- There was a corporate merger.
- I raised my family.
- I wanted a job requiring my best skills.
- I began self-employment.
- There was a general layoff in the plant.
- I wanted to be more productive.
- The work was seasonal.
- The work was part-time.
- The company was closing.
- I preferred a better work environment.
- I was doing volunteer work.
- I wanted a job in which I could learn.
- There was a lack of operating funds within the company.
- I became a full-time student.
- I made a long-planned move to this area.
- I began a long-planned tour of the country.
- I took an extended vacation.

Quick Tip!

If you left your former job for any of the negative reasons listed above, you can look at the positive reasons for leaving list to see if you might be able to choose a much better option to answer an interview question with!

Example interview question script

You may use this employment script as an example for your practice interviews and change the questions to fit the needs of your particular job or career environment.
Include your own personal tough questions!

1. *Tell me a little about yourself.*
2. *What do you know about my company?*
3. *What is your main form of transportation?*
4. *If hired, will you be keeping any other jobs while working here?*
5. *Describe yourself as to what kind of worker you are.*
6. *Describe yourself as your friends would.*
7. *Describe a rare work quality about yourself.*
8. *Why are you changing fields?*
9. *Why is there a job gap in your work history?*
10. *If you were to describe yourself in three words what would they be?*
11. *Describe what your duties were at your most recent job.*
12. *Why are you applying for this position?*
13. *How do you spend your free time?*
14. *Are you willing to relocate?*
15. *Why are you leaving your present job?*
16. *What are your greatest accomplishments at work regarding customer service?*
17. *What was your most serious problem at work that you've dealt with?*
18. *Describe the ideal job for you.*
19. *Where do you see yourself in five years?*
20. *If I asked your former employer, what would they likely say about you?*
21. *Describe how your education fits into this position.*
22. *What skills are you bringing to this position?*
23. *Why should I hire you over anyone else?*
24. *Do you have any questions for me?*

Chapter 8

Keeping the Job

BE SURE TO STOP AND CELEBRATE YOUR ACCOMPLISHMENTS!

Enjoy the job or career you have chosen!

You are the person who chose to apply at the company initially so smile and enjoy your time at work as much as possible! You ARE getting paid!

Be trustworthy at your job

It may sound simple but you will work up the ladder much faster, get more raises and be trusted with jobs that are important to the employer and need to be entrusted to someone who would do the job in the same way as the manager/owner would him/herself. To a good manager, this is priceless!

Pay attention to the specific details and rules of the job

Follow ALL directions! Read all of the instructions before filling out paperwork. Again, sounds simple but you would not believe how many people I see simply forget to take half a minute and read the instructions, as well as simply listening to instructions! It is very frustrating for an employer to be near done with his sentence and the employee cuts the employer off and says, "Oh yea, I got It," so the employer leaves them alone trusting that they know how to do it and then the job is not done correctly. Even the smallest details always matter!

Take care of yourself during and after all that work!

Laughter releases stress at work. We need to be serious enough to get the job done but at the same time loose enough to enjoy our working day. That will get you through your working day. Then when you get home, take care of yourself. This is the greatest gift you could give yourself after work. If you find that you have no time to do anything fun to release your stress you really aren't living to your fullest potential. Plus, when you are rested you work better the next day! When you get away from the problems at work mentally you create an extremely necessary oasis for yourself!

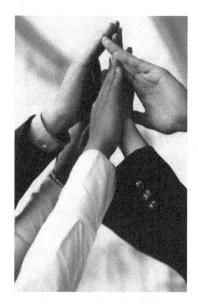

Team Player?

Are you really a team player? If your co-worker got the job you wanted are you still happy for them or do you walk around showing everyone what a bad choice you think that was? Remember, your employers are actually seeing your reaction even if you don't think they are. Also, remember that they are the ones who chose the other person for the promotion in the first place. If you want the next promotion, be truly happy for the advancement of your co-worker and offer them help with whatever they need. This person may be the one to call you when a new promotion comes up!

Be polite to your co-workers

Don't let yourself fall for gossip games. It's really easy for coworkers to want to vent to each other about someone in the workplace. This is okay and healthy to a point to release those emotions- on the rare occasion but it's best to release the tension with people at home! When talking about someone's character, it can always come back to bite you in the office. Gossip can ruin your chances of advancement and is just plain petty. Even if you agree with what is being said, I would seriously suggest saying something like, "Oh really? I've never seen that side of her," or "She's always been very nice to me."

If you choose to say anything other than a very direct positive statement, the bent co-worker can twist what you said into saying that you agreed with him or her about what was said about the other person. Not good! This can burn a bridge even if you're just being a "shoulder" for someone. Remember, you all work for the same company and are all therefore working for the same ultimate goals.

Don't date at work

If you possibly can, try to make it a rule for yourself because if things don't work out between the two of you, work can get pretty uncomfortable at times for you and your co-workers as well! Remember, you still have to "work" together. Also, it's a good idea to make it a rule not to date your clients as well. Mixing business with pleasure can not only make things awkward sometimes, but it could also cost you your job!

Back it up!

Always use an alarm clock with a backup battery in case of power failure. This is really not the best excuse for coming in late anymore as employers know that power failures do happen and you as an employee must be prepared.

Show your loyalty!

Employers want loyal employees that they can count on and don't have to worry about. They know that these choice employees will make sure the job is done as they want it done, even when the bosses are away. You can show your loyalty in a variety of ways such as: Completing your assigned tasks to the best of your abilities, not wasting time on the clock, taking on extra responsibilities when someone is ill or on vacation, etc.

YOUR BOSS

Sadly, I hear so many people say that they absolutely do not like their bosses. You may have some great reasons but come on now, your employer essentially feeds you. You should never hate them and if you do, you may want to find other employment for your own sake. Only you can be responsible for your destiny. You don't deserve to stay in that type of environment if it becomes that hostile. In a normal, healthy setting, you should acknowledge your boss's presence when they walk into the room. Why not try to make him or her have a better day?

What is it worth to you to do the opposite? Is looking down or away when they walk in the room worth losing your job? If so, keep your eyes out for other employment now while you're still there because humans pick up on negative body language fairly quickly as it is instinctive. Does looking down or away show honesty to them? Probably not! Even if you're the most honest employee they have, you can, through your body language, make them think you are hiding something or that you are avoiding them for some reason and any person with a decent amount of intelligence will want to try to figure out why.

Get to know your bosses!
They are human too, and I can
guarantee that the more you know
about them, the more similarities that
you will see between them and
yourself and who knows?
You may just learn to like them!

Criticism

There are two types of criticism, constructive and destructive. You should never be demeaned or dishonored. If you are not experiencing this type of criticism, you may have supervisors that respect you and only wish to criticize constructively, which is their job to do essentially when needed. If you are being criticized, consider if this criticism would be something you would have to bring up with another employee if you were in the supervisors position.

Sometimes the hardest part about supervising others is that you will have to criticize individual performance. Sometimes it is hard to take criticism as well. The key is to try not to let it affect you emotionally. Every supervisor has different ways of delivering the information but if you are experiencing constructive criticism, understand where they are coming from and allow the change to take effect in you and then get back to doing the job you love!

211

Look closely at your past work experiences and learn from them!

This may be a painful process but well worth it to ask yourself these questions and write down your answers on the next page.

Why did I hate my boss?
Could I have looked at the same situation from his/her point of view and seen more clearly what he/she needed from me?
Do I tend to gossip or backbite in the workplace?
Do I put in an honest day's work?
Do I slack or say "I can't wait to get home!" often?
What is my most difficult characteristic that a co-worker would need to deal with when working closely with me?
Do I praise my co-workers when they advance?
Am I considered a team player to my co-workers?
Do I come to work with a smile?
Do I expect other people to make me happy?

When you find out the true reasons why maybe previous employment experiences didn't work out, you can learn from them and better yourself in the process!

Write your answers to the questions on the previous page in this box:

Remember, once you understand where you have been and why, and figure out where you want to be and why, you will be able to accomplish any interview session successfully. You may even have to turn a few extra offers down!

Employer's perspective

Your individual personality has a place and has validity to an employer who needs your unique abilities. Have you ever been offered new employment while working at a job? It's happened to me a few times and it used to offend me because I was always working at a job that I loved at the time and someone was trying to take me away to new employment. It sometimes got to where people would follow me from store to store and would keep coming in to offer employment. I never considered it a compliment as my bosses would always be near and I was always afraid that they would think that I solicited these people to come around! I started to understand why they did this, some call them headhunters, but most are regular employers keeping their eye out for good people for their business while doing their regular daily routine.

They were recruiting and I was showing my love for my work, wherever I worked. That is enticing to any employer! If you are multitasking and being efficient and still have a smile on your face- hmmm... rarity. Get the picture? Luckily my bosses knew who I was and my worth to them and now I just take it as a compliment and politely let the headhunters know that I had the best job in the world and that I loved my job and the people I worked with. I tell you this to remind you to start looking at employees from an employers' perspective. When they see what they need, they want to have it to better their business.

They see it as a great fit and they are intelligent enough to try their best to get their needs met through individuals that they invite to do the work that they cannot do for themselves. They want someone to represent them, as if they themselves were working that job. They *need* that. If you don't carry the same values that the employer is looking for, you are not going to be the right fit for them. In the same way that you can tell when someone loves their work, you can also tell when someone absolutely hates it as well. You have to have a general love for work even though we all have those tough days. This will give you inner peace.

We spend a lot of our time at work-
Try to make the best of it for your own sanity!

Congratulations!
You have completed the course!

Once you get the job you want, (And you will!) stay positive at work. Stay self-motivated and looking, acting like, and truly becoming a team player. There is nothing worse than one person with a bad attitude to affect everyone's day. If you stay positive, you will always have a good reference from that company which can be very valuable to you later!

ENJOY YOUR LIFE

ENJOY YOUR WORK!

Suggested reading and acknowledgments

DRESS FOR SUCCESS
By, John T. Molloy

JOB HUNTERS:
PACKAGING AND MARKETING YOU
By, Barney Ramos

KNOW YOUR STRENGTHS AND BE CONFIDENT
By, Iris Barrow

THE 10 DUMBEST MISTAKES SMART PEOPLE MAKE
AND HOW TO AVOID THEM
By, Dr. Arthur Freeman
& Rose DeWolf

FEELING GOOD
THE NEW MOOD THERAPY
By, David D. Burns MD

HOW TO WIN FRIENDS AND INFLUENCE PEOPLE
By, Dale Carnegie

101 GREAT ANSWERS TO THE TOUGHEST INTERVIEW
QUESTIONS
By, Ron Fry

THE WORKBOOK
GETTING THE JOB YOU WANT
By, J. Michael Farr,
Richard Gaither & R. Michael Pickrell

COLOR ME BEAUTIFUL'S
LOOKING YOUR BEST
COLOR, MAKEUP AND STYLE
By Mary Spillane & Christine Sherlock

RESUMES THAT KNOCK 'EM DEAD
By, Martin Yate

Printed in the United States
By Bookmasters